more from
the accidental vegetarian

simon rimmer

more from
the accidental vegetarian

MITCHELL BEAZLEY

MORE FROM THE ACCIDENTAL VEGETARIAN
by Simon Rimmer

Previously published as Seasoned Vegetarian
by Simon Rimmer

First published in Great Britain in 2009 by Mitchell Beazley,
an imprint of Octopus Publishing Group Ltd,
Endeavour House, 189 Shaftesbury Avenue, London, WC2H 8JY
www.octopusbooks.co.uk

An Hachette UK Company
www.hachette.co.uk

First published in paperback in 2012

Copyright © Octopus Publishing Group Ltd 2012
Photographs copyright © Chris Terry 2012

ISBN: 978 1 84533 673 8

A CIP record for this book is available from the British Library.

Set in Scala and Scala Sans

Colour reproduction by Sang Choy in Singapore
Printed and bound in China

Commissioning Editor Rebecca Spry
Art Director Tim Foster
Project Editor Leanne Bryan
Editor Maggie Pannell
Proofreader Jo Murray
Indexer Helen Snaith
Executive Art Editors Pene Parker & Yasia Williams-Leedham
Designer Nicky Collings
Photographer Chris Terry
Senior Production Controller Lucy Carter

*For AliMac, who somehow puts up
with me and my numerous faults.*

contents

INTRODUCTION

There's been a lot of water under the bridge since I wrote *The Accidental Vegetarian*. I'm older, wiser? (probably not) and my kids have grown up too fast – no longer my little babies, but a strapping 5-year-old Hamish and a 10-year-old, going on 15-year-old, Flo!

Food-wise, finally it seems the world has realised that British food and produce is *bloody* brilliant: artisan cheesemakers, asparagus growers, rare-breed farmers, fruit and juice producers, not to mention restaurants, delis, pubs and micro-breweries. In fact, it's a great time to be involved with anything foodie in our great land.

Now, veggie food, or meat-free, as I think it's becoming known, is really changing. When we opened Greens in 1990, nearly all veggie food was either brown and worthy in many vegetarian eateries, or a cheese salad in non-vegetarian haunts. In case you didn't know, I opened Greens with no knowledge of cooking, just two cookery books and a guilty secret of being a devout carnivore! Once we got going I wanted to have a restaurant that people would regard in the same way as, say, going for an Indian meal: 'I'm not Indian but I love Indian food' (substitute the word 'vegetarian' for 'Indian' and you get the picture). So, over the course of our 18 years we've created just such a place with over 65 per cent of our customers being carnivores. And, joyously, non-veggie restaurants now do great meat-free dishes, a world away from the cheese salad, as vegetarian cuisine has come out of the shadows and into the light!

So, this follow-on book is really more of the same: simple, tasty food that everyone can enjoy, and I've even reinvented the nut loaf! So dust off the cheesecloth and sandals and dig in.

brunch

sweet figs on toast

Feeds 4

You know those things you used to make as a kid – sugar butties? Bread, butter and sugar...yum yum! Sooooo bad for you, yet delicious! Well this is really a more adult version of that, but I've disguised the 'badness' with figs and ricotta.

Brush the bread with the oil, then griddle until well lined with char-grill markings.

Beat the ricotta with the spices and cayenne pepper.

Spread the ricotta on the bread and lay the figs on the top. Splash a tiny amount of vinegar on them, then sprinkle with sugar.

Place the toasts under a medium-hot grill and toast until the sugar caramelises.

Eat them with relish as though you're a small child and it's your birthday!

8 slices sourdough bread
oil, for brushing bread
300g (10oz) ricotta cheese
1 tsp ground nutmeg
1 tsp ground cinnamon
pinch of cayenne pepper
8 fresh figs, sliced
dash of sherry vinegar
caster sugar, for grilling

hotcakes with blueberry butter

Feeds 4
(makes 8–12 pancakes)

My kids go absolutely crazy for hotcakes, which are also called griddle cakes or American pancakes. In fact, Hamish would eat them morning, noon and night if given the chance. I'm not suggesting for a second that these are healthy, but at least the blueberries will provide you with one portion of your daily fruit intake. Great served with maple syrup.

First make the blueberry butter. Gently heat the blueberries, lemon juice and sugar in a pan for around 6–8 minutes until the blueberries begin to break down. Remove the pan from the heat and leave to cool.

Meanwhile, beat the butter until pale and fluffy, then quickly whisk in the blueberry mixture until the butter looks marbled. Put in the fridge to chill.

For the pancakes, beat together the ricotta, milk, egg yolks and sugar until smooth. Sift in the flour, baking powder and salt.

Whisk the egg whites until quite stiff, then fold them into the pancake batter.

Melt a knob of butter in a griddle or frying pan, spoon in large, heaped spoonfuls of the batter, spacing them well apart and cook for 2 minutes on each side until golden and firm.

Remove the pancake from the pan and keep warm while cooking the rest of the pancakes, lightly greasing the pan with a little more butter between each batch.

Stack up the pancakes and serve topped with a generous spoonful of the blueberry butter and plenty of maple syrup.

Blueberry butter
175g (6oz) blueberries
juice of 1 lemon
50g (2oz) caster sugar
75g (3oz) unsalted butter

Pancakes
250g (9oz) ricotta cheese, drained
125ml (4fl oz) milk
3 eggs, separated
50g (2oz) caster sugar
100g (3½oz) plain flour
1 tsp baking powder
pinch of salt
butter, for frying
maple syrup, to serve

melon, mint & coconut smoothie

Feeds 4

1 melon (be it watermelon,
  honeydew or cantaloupe),
  deseeded and cubed
400ml can coconut milk
large handful of fresh mint
lots of ice
splash of coconut liqueur
  (optional)

So easy, simply blend the melon in a food processor with everything else until smooth and serve in chilled glasses. That's it!

The Simpsons are a bit of a feature in our house – so much so, that one of my son Hamish's first words was 'Homer'! My favourite line from the show is when Krusty the Clown calls honeydew melon 'the money melon'. Honeydew works a treat in this smoothie, but it's great with a sweet orange cantaloupe too. The choice is yours. If you're having a party, why not make a smoothie with each type for colour variation?

crunchy eggs

Feeds 1

75g (3oz) fresh breadcrumbs
salt and freshly ground black
  pepper
50ml (2fl oz) olive oil
2 eggs
1 tbsp sherry vinegar
splash of hot chilli sauce

Put the breadcrumbs and seasoning in a warm frying pan, add about half the oil, then cook for 3–4 minutes on a medium heat until the crumbs begin to dry out.

Add the rest of the oil, stir well, then crack the eggs on top and cook to perfection.

Slide the eggs on to a plate and add the vinegar and chilli sauce to the hot pan. Shake it around then pour the hot vinegar and chilli sauce on top of the eggs.

I had these babies in San Francisco a few years ago and they've become a real favourite of mine. Great food can come in many forms, and I always like it when a dish can both satisfy and amuse me at the same time, like this one.

px mushrooms on toast

Feeds 4

PX is a sherry, but it is unlike any other sherry in the world. Imagine the taste of Christmas pudding mixed with a bit of chocolate and spice...and there you have it. It's made by Fernando de Castilla and I think it's ace. Combine it with some earthy wild mushrooms and slap 'em on toast with a rub of garlic and suddenly the world is an altogether better place.

Heat the oil and butter in a frying pan until the butter begins to foam.

Add the mushrooms to the pan. Let them sit for a couple of minutes, then begin to move them around. Add the garlic and season well.

Once the mushrooms are soft, after about 5 minutes, add the lemon juice and cook for 1 minute.

Next add the PX, crank up the heat and cook for 3 minutes to reduce the liquid a little. Just before serving, stir in the thyme.

Serve on top of char-grilled or toasted sourdough bread, which has been drizzled with oil and rubbed with garlic.

2 tbsp olive oil

75g (3oz) butter

450g (1lb) mushrooms (wild are good or, failing that, use fresh shiitakes, portobellos or chestnut), sliced or roughly chopped

1 garlic clove, crushed

salt and freshly ground black pepper

juice of ½ lemon

125ml (4fl oz) PX sherry

1 tbsp fresh thyme leaves

To serve

4 thick slices sourdough bread, griddled or toasted

50ml (2fl oz) extra-virgin olive oil

1 garlic clove, halved

spinach & potato omelette with salted *padrón* chillies

Feeds 4

Salted *padrón* chillies
100ml (3½ fl oz) olive oil, for frying the chillies
30 *padrón* chillies
sea salt, to toss

Omelette
6 eggs
75ml (2½ fl oz) double cream
salt and freshly ground black pepper
2–3 tbsp olive oil, for frying
1 large onion, sliced
1 garlic clove, crushed
125g (4½ oz) baby spinach
125g (4½ oz) cooked potatoes, cubed
chopped tomatoes, to garnish

Heat the olive oil in a frying pan. When hot, add the whole chillies, including the stalks and cook until their skins blister. Drain on kitchen paper, then toss in a little sea salt and set aside.

For the omelette, beat the eggs with the cream and seasoning until the mixture is fluffy.

Heat the oil in a large frying pan, add the onion and garlic and fry over a medium heat until soft and just beginning to caramelise.

Add the spinach and potatoes to the pan and cook for 2 minutes.

Pour in the egg mixture and stir until the omelette begins to set around the edge. Now gently whisk the surface with a fork to help it cook, tipping any uncooked egg from the centre of the omelette around the edge of the pan.

Once the omelette is three-quarters set, pop the pan under a hot grill to finish cooking it.

Serve a good wedge of the omelette with the chillies and garnish with some chopped tomatoes.

The chillies provided the inspiration for this recipe. *Padrón* chillies are little beauties – small, tasty and fiery, they go brilliantly well with this simple omelette. They came to my attention because of a nutter called Rich, who grows chillies in Chorley, Lancashire, and makes chilli cheese and chilli beer. He put me on to them and deservedly is now (in my kingdom) Lord Chilli of Chorley!

breakfast burrito

Feeds 4

On holiday in Santa Cruz I used to go to a great little Mexican place called the Sunshine Café for breakfast. It was just around the corner from where I was staying and had loads of alfresco seating. Although it looked a bit grotty from the outside I applied the 'Rimmer Rule': as there was a constant stream of customers I decided it must be either very good or very cheap. In fact, it was both. Now, I've had breakfast burritos many times before, but the ones I tasted in Santa Cruz were the business. Try to search out soft corn tortillas as they make a real difference.

Preheat the oven to 200°C/Fan 180°C/Gas 6. Put the red peppers in a roasting tin, brush with a little oil and roast for about 15 minutes until softened. Place the peppers in a plastic bag and leave to sweat until they are cool enough to handle. Remove the peppers from the bag and peel off the skins, cut in half and remove the seeds. Reduce the oven temperature to 180°C/Fan 160°C/Gas 4.

Stack the tortillas and wrap them in foil, then place them in the oven to warm for 10 minutes, or according to the packet instructions.

Beat the eggs with the milk and seasoning. Melt the butter in a large non-stick frying pan and, as it begins to foam, pour in the egg mixture. Do not touch the eggs until they just begin to set, then, once they do, move them gently towards the centre of the pan with a spatula. Continue to cook until they're set, flip over using the spatula, then remove from the heat.

Roughly chop both types of peppers along with the cooked spinach.

To assemble the burrito, place a quarter of the cheese on one side of the tortilla, then top with a quarter of the spinach and pepper mixture, then a quarter of the eggs. Roll up tightly and eat immediately served with super-hot Jamaican sauce.

3 red peppers
1 tbsp oil, for roasting
4 soft corn tortillas
  (flour tortillas will do if corn
  tortillas are unavailable)
6 eggs
6 tbsp milk
salt and freshly ground black
  pepper
1 tbsp butter
6 Pepperdew peppers
  (drained from a jar)
2 tbsp cooked baby spinach,
  squeezed of excess water
100g (3½ oz) Manchego or
  mature Cheddar cheese, grated
hot Jamaican sauce, to serve

soups&salads

green veggie soup with egg

Feeds 4

I sometimes think that soup recipes are a bit of a cheat in books – pumpkin, pea, mushroom... they all have the same basic principles of cooking. But this recipe, and the White gazpacho (see page 26), are fabulous soups that are different in technique and flavour from the norm, and therefore deserve a place in the book. This beauty is so delicious I suggest doubling the quantities because you'll want to serve it again straight away.

Heat some oil in a saucepan, add the onions and celery and fry until soft over a low heat. Add the courgettes, potatoes and lemon zest.

Stir for a couple of minutes, then add the stock and bring to the boil. Add the beans, then reduce the heat and simmer for 15 minutes.

Add the lettuce and spinach and simmer for a further 5 minutes, or until the potatoes are cooked. Season to taste.

Beat the eggs and lemon juice together, then stir into the simmering soup. Cook for just 1 minute, then ladle the soup into bowls. Scatter some cheese on top and garnish with sprigs of watercress.

oil, for frying
6 spring onions, finely chopped
3 celery sticks, chopped
250g (9oz) courgettes, cut into bite-sized chunks
350g (12oz) potatoes, peeled and cubed
juice and grated zest of 1 lemon
1.5 litres (2½ pints) vegetable stock
100g (3½oz) shelled broad beans
1 head Little Gem lettuce, shredded
handful of baby spinach
salt and freshly ground black pepper
2 eggs
grated pecorino cheese, to serve
watercress sprigs, to garnish

bean broth with sage dumplings

Feeds 4

A simple, delicious broth that gets a big hearty visitor from Mr Sage Dumpling. I really love sage, but it can be a little bit medicinal, so if you prefer to use a different herb, I won't be offended. Serve with lots of crusty bread and unsalted butter.

Heat the oil in a large saucepan, add the onion and garlic and fry for about 5 minutes until soft.

Add the rest of the broth ingredients, except the tomatoes, and bring to the boil. Turn down the heat to a simmer and allow to cook gently for 30 minutes, until the barley is almost tender.

For the dumplings, stir together the flour, suet, sage and a pinch of salt, then add 3–4 tablespoons of cold water to bind the mixture into a soft dough.

Divide the dough into even pieces and roll into about 16 small dumplings, using a little flour.

Drop the dumplings into the broth and simmer for 15–20 minutes.

Finally, gently stir the tomatoes into the broth, warm through, then serve immediately.

Broth
1 tbsp vegetable oil, for frying
1 onion, chopped
1 garlic clove, crushed
400ml (14fl oz) vegetable stock
125g (4½oz) pearl barley
grated zest and juice of 1 lemon
400g can butter beans, drained and rinsed
salt and freshly ground black pepper
4 plum tomatoes, chopped

Sage dumplings
100g (3½oz) self-raising flour
50g (2oz) shredded vegetable suet
2 tbsp chopped fresh sage

hot & sour soup

Feeds 4

1 litre (1¾ pints) vegetable stock
4 garlic cloves, crushed
2.5cm (1-inch) piece fresh root
   ginger, cut into matchsticks
1 lemongrass stalk, bruised
1 tbsp light soy sauce
1 birds eye chilli, finely chopped
1 tbsp rice vinegar
1 tbsp brown sugar
2 kaffir lime leaves
juice of 1 lime
200g (7oz) deep-fried tofu,
   chopped into cubes
100g (3½oz) oyster
   mushrooms, sliced
1 red pepper, sliced
150g (5oz) bok choy, chopped
2 eggs
salt and freshly ground black
   pepper
fresh basil leaves, to garnish
chilli sauce and lime wedges,
   to serve

Bring the stock to the boil in a large saucepan, then add the garlic, ginger, lemongrass, soy, chilli, vinegar, sugar, kaffir lime leaves and lime juice. Simmer for 5 minutes.

Add the tofu, mushrooms, red pepper and bok choy and cook for another 4 minutes.

Beat the eggs in a cup, then slide them into the soup and stir gently.

Check the seasoning, then ladle the soup into deep bowls, scatter basil leaves and a few drops of chilli sauce over the top and serve with lime wedges.

To my mind this is one of the best soups in the world and a real pick-me-up. It's sharp and spicy and, at the same time, warming, refreshing and filling. It's a soup that four people can eat and each can get something different from it. If you want the egg to be in small threads, keep stirring when it goes in; if you want it more like a fluffy cloud, stir only once.

oyster mushroom & tofu laksa

Feeds 4

2 red chillies, deseeded

25g (1oz) fresh root ginger, peeled and roughly chopped

2 garlic cloves

1 lemongrass stalk, trimmed, outer layer removed and chopped

1 tsp coriander seeds, dry-fried and ground

few sprigs fresh coriander

1 tbsp tamarind sauce

50ml (2fl oz) vegetable oil

250g (9oz) plum tomatoes, roughly chopped

500ml (18fl oz) vegetable stock

400ml can coconut milk

125g (4½oz) tofu, cut into big chunks

250g (9oz) oyster mushrooms, thinly sliced

1 tbsp light soy sauce

200g (7oz) medium-thick egg noodles

chopped spring onions, mint leaves, sliced red chillies and lime wedges, to serve

Put the chillies, ginger, garlic, lemongrass, coriander seeds, fresh coriander, tamarind sauce and oil in a food processor and blend to a smooth paste.

Fry the paste in a wok until it becomes aromatic.

Add the tomatoes and cook for 5 minutes, then add the stock and coconut milk and bring to the boil.

Add the tofu, mushrooms and soy sauce and simmer gently for 4 minutes.

Meanwhile, cook the egg noodles in boiling water for 4 minutes, or according to the packet instructions. Drain and divide between four deep bowls.

Ladle the spicy coconut broth over the top of the noodles. Serve garnished with spring onions and mint leaves and accompanied by lime wedges, so that diners can squeeze the juice into their soup.

If you've never had a laksa before, let me tempt you: it's a cross between a soup, a curry and a noodle dish, always aromatic, sometimes spicy and very, very satisfying. This beauty is one of the few dishes I use tofu in, and it's delicious. It's also considered bad manners if you don't slurp loudly when eating to get lots of oxygen in your mouth to bring out the flavour – all together now!

white gazpacho

Feeds 4

I'd never heard of white gazpacho until we did a wedding for a couple at Greens a few years back and they wanted it as an inter-course. So I did the research, found a few variations and became hooked on this wonderful fresh soup – and NO you can't have it warm.

Put the almonds in a food processor and blend until as fine as possible.

Add about 50ml (2fl oz) of the water and blend to a smooth paste.

Now add the bread and garlic and blend again.

Add the rest of the water with the food processor motor running, then the olive oil.

Finally add the vinegar and seasoning to taste.

Divide the soup evenly between four bowls, drizzle with olive oil and scatter the raisins on top to garnish.

250g (9oz) whole blanched almonds
500ml (18fl oz) iced water
75g (3oz) white bread, crusts removed and cubed
2 garlic cloves
50ml (2fl oz) extra-virgin olive oil, plus extra to garnish
50ml (2fl oz) sherry vinegar
salt and freshly ground black pepper
150g (5oz) golden raisins, to garnish (soak these in a little brandy, if liked)

broad bean salad with manchego & mint

Feeds 4–6

The Italians do magnificent things with broad beans, and early season fresh beans are a joy to behold. Then the Spanish do great things with Manchego cheese, which has become such a favourite of mine in recent years. They BOTH do brilliant things with lemons and olive oil, so this is a celebration of the genius of both countries and their food. Serve with a selection of yummy breads.

Place the shelled beans in a saucepan and cover with boiling water. Bring back to the boil, then reduce the heat, cover and simmer gently for about 5 minutes, until the beans are just tender.

Drain the beans, toss in the olive oil and season. I like to let them sit in the oil for a good 10 minutes before serving the salad.

When you're ready to serve, add the lemon juice, then toss in the cheese, mint leaves and watercress.

1.8kg (4lb) fresh broad beans, shelled
100ml (3½ fl oz) good quality extra-virgin olive oil
salt and freshly ground black pepper
juice of 1 lemon
125g (4½ oz) Manchego cheese, finely sliced
1 tbsp fresh mint leaves, roughly chopped
bunch of watercress, trimmed

feta & watermelon salad

Feeds 4

When the weather's good, I like nothing more than a simple salad with a cheeky glass of something cold and fizzy. This fits the bill to perfection – sweet, juicy watermelon with tangy feta cheese and a cider vinegar dressing to marry them together.

Cut the watermelon in half lengthways and scoop out the middle, then cut the flesh into 2.5cm (1-inch) chunks, discarding the seeds. Cut the cucumber in half lengthways and then slice it thickly into half moons. Transfer to a large salad bowl with the rest of the salad ingredients.

Whisk together all the ingredients for the dressing, seasoning to taste.

Drizzle the dressing sparingly over the salad, toss together and serve immediately. You'll probably have some dressing left over, which can be saved for another salad, in a screw-top jar in the fridge.

½ watermelon
1 cucumber
250g (9oz) Greek feta cheese, cubed
about 24 stoned black olives, preferably Greek Kalamata
handful of rocket
2 toasted pitta breads, torn up into bite-sized pieces

Dressing
300ml (½ pint) extra-virgin olive oil
100ml (3½ fl oz) cider vinegar
2.5cm (1-inch) piece fresh root ginger, peeled and grated
2 tbsp chopped fresh mint
juice of ½ lime
salt and freshly ground black pepper

black pudding & stilton salad

Feeds 4

250g (9oz) vegetarian black
 pudding, cut into 2.5cm
 (1-inch) thick rounds
1–2 tbsp oil, for frying
175g (6oz) Stilton cheese
handful of rocket
100g (3½oz) cooked peas
1 tbsp pine nuts, toasted
Little Gem lettuce, to serve

Dressing
1 tbsp Dijon mustard
juice and grated zest of
 ½ orange
1 tbsp cider vinegar
100ml (3½fl oz) olive oil
salt and freshly ground black
 pepper

Fry the rounds of veggie black pudding in oil for about 2 minutes on each side until crisp. Drain on kitchen paper.

Meanwhile, cut the Stilton into cubes and put into a bowl with the rocket, peas and pine nuts.

Whisk together all the ingredients for the dressing.

Add the black pudding to the salad, then some dressing. Toss and check the seasoning.

Separate the lettuce into its individual leaves and arrange on serving plates, then pile the salad on top.

Andy Holt is a bit of a genius and, much as it galls me to say it, the man has created one of the best vegetarian products of recent times: his veggie black pudding. Andy is a 'blood and guts' kind of guy, who makes award-winning traditional black puddings, but his incredible veggie version uses beetroot juice and whey powder for the 'blood'. Since I became hooked on it, we always have something featuring it on the Greens menu. This salad combines the sweetness of the black pudding with the acidity of Stilton and marries them with a yummy citrus dressing. Oh, and Andy, you still owe me a pint! Serve with either sun-dried tomato or walnut bread.

honey griddled aubergine with fennel & orange salad

Feeds 4

This is a really delicious salad that combines sweetened aubergine with the fruity acidity of orange and fennel. I really think the radicchio works brilliantly here, giving a bitter edge to the dish. Serve with some warmed flat bread.

Toss the aubergine wedges in oil, then griddle for 1 minute on each side until lined with char markings. Meanwhile, heat the honey and soy sauce together. Toss the char-grilled aubergines in this dressing.

Toss together the fennel, orange segments and juice with the olive oil. Arrange the radicchio in a serving bowl. Shake off any excess dressing from the aubergines, then toss them with the fennel and oranges. Pile on top of the radicchio.

Garnish with snipped chives scattered over the top.

2 aubergines, cut into wedges
oil, to coat the aubergines
3 tbsp honey
1 tsp light soy sauce
1 fennel bulb, sliced very thinly
2 oranges, segmented, any juice retained
50ml (2fl oz) extra-virgin olive oil
1 head radicchio, broken into individual leaves
snipped chives, to garnish

pear & fennel salad with garlic walnut paste

Feeds 4

I use Bosc pears in this recipe; they're those greeny-brown ones that are always a bit crunchy and truly delectable. Their freshness is a delight with the fennel, then it gets a right lashing with the walnut paste (based on a classic French *aillade*) and a squirt of balsamic vinegar for good measure – absolutely delicious.

To make the *aillade*, simply blitz all the ingredients together in a food processor until smooth.

For the salad, use a mandolin to slice the fennel and pears very thinly.

Put a small spoonful of the walnut paste in the centre of each serving plate and press flat.

Layer up the fennel and pears on top of the paste, sit more paste on top, then drizzle with oil and balsamic vinegar and top with pecorino shavings.

Walnut paste (*aillade*)
75g (3oz) walnuts
2 garlic cloves
grated zest of ½ orange
30ml (1fl oz) brandy
salt and freshly ground black pepper

Salad
1 fennel bulb, trimmed
1–2 Bosc pears
100ml (3½fl oz) extra-virgin olive oil
75ml (2½fl oz) aged balsamic vinegar
100g (3½oz) pecorino cheese shavings

pumpkin salad with cheese

Feeds 6

3–4 tbsp olive oil, for roasting
300g (10oz) pumpkin, peeled
    and cut into bite-sized cubes
salt and freshly ground black
    pepper
200g (7oz) fettle cheese, cubed
150g (5oz) pine nuts, toasted
handful each of watercress,
    rocket and baby spinach
3 radishes, sliced
150g (5oz) peas, cooked

Dressing
150ml (¼ pint) extra-virgin
    olive oil
juice of 2 limes
1 tbsp cider vinegar
1 tbsp chopped fresh mint
1 garlic clove, crushed

Preheat the oven to 200°C/Fan 180°C/Gas 6. Heat the oil in a roasting tin, add the pumpkin and roast for about 30 minutes until golden and soft. Drain on kitchen paper and season well.

Combine the pumpkin with the rest of the salad ingredients in a large bowl.

Make the dressing by putting all the ingredients in a screw-top jar and shaking it up like crazy.

Drizzle the dressing over the salad and toss all of it together, then serve.

From the moment this dish went on the menu it has sold like hot cakes (a strange comparison, I know). Yorkshire fettle cheese, from Shepherd's Purse creamery, is a great example of how brilliant British cheesemakers are. This cheese has all the characteristics of a feta, with the added oomph of a Wensleydale. Combined with sweet pumpkin, pine nuts and the rest, it makes for a good year-round salad.

smoked pistachio, artichoke & potato salad

Feeds 4

16 new potatoes, scrubbed
8 canned artichokes, drained
olive oil, for brushing artichokes
1 red onion, halved, then sliced
100g (3½oz) smoked pistachios
1 tbsp chopped fresh dill
4 tbsp cottage cheese

Dressing
200ml (7fl oz) extra-virgin
    olive oil
50ml (2fl oz) sherry vinegar
juice of ½ lemon
salt and freshly ground black
    pepper

Cook the potatoes in a pan of salted boiling water for about 15 minutes until tender, then drain, cool and thickly slice.

Brush the artichokes with the oil, then cook on a preheated griddle until well charred.

For the dressing, put the oil, vinegar, lemon juice and seasoning in a screw-top jar and shake well together.

To serve, toss the potatoes, artichokes, onion, nuts and dill in the dressing. Pile on to plates and top with cottage cheese.

My favourite restaurant in the whole world is the Spotted Pig in Greenwich Village, New York. It's a crazy, mad, busy place that serves simple food, well cooked. One of the best things I've ever eaten there was a smoked trout salad with cottage cheese – much like this, but I'm using smoked nuts rather than fish. Just thinking about 'the pig' makes me want to go back to New York NOW!

smallplatefuls

asparagus spears with pecorino shortbread

Feeds 8

This is one of my favourite starters on the menu at Greens. The combination is a joy to eat; first there's the crunch and crispness of the shortbread, and then there's the sharp dressing and the peppery rocket and earthy asparagus, which are all topped off with the salty shavings of pecorino cheese.

First make the dressing. Put the egg yolks, sugar, mustard, vinegar, lemon juice and seasoning in a food processor and mix together. Slowly add the oil, with the motor running, then finally add the tarragon. Transfer into a bowl and set aside.

To make the shortbread, pulse the flour and butter in the cleaned food processor until they look like damp breadcrumbs. Add the cheese and seasoning, then bind with the egg yolk.

Preheat the oven to 180°C/Fan 160°C/Gas 4.

Roll out the shortbread on a lightly floured surface and cut into 16 triangles, each one measuring about 10 x 7.5 x 7.5cm (4 x 3 x 3 inches).

Place the shortbread triangles on a baking sheet and bake for 8 minutes, or until golden. Meanwhile, steam the asparagus spears for 8–10 minutes, or until just tender.

Toss the asparagus spears with the rocket and dressing in a large bowl.

To serve, place a shortbread triangle on each plate, sit the asparagus and rocket salad on top, allowing three spears for each serving. Scatter with pecorino shavings and another piece of crunchy shortbread.

24 asparagus spears, trimmed
large handful of rocket
pecorino cheese shavings,
   to garnish

Dressing
2 egg yolks
4 tsp caster sugar
2 tsp Dijon mustard
75ml (2½ fl oz) white wine
   vinegar
juice of 1 lemon
salt and freshly ground black
   pepper
300ml (½ pint) olive oil
1 tbsp chopped fresh tarragon

Shortbread
175g (6oz) plain flour, plus extra
   for dusting
100g (3½oz) cold butter, cubed
65g (2½oz) pecorino cheese,
   finely grated
salt and freshly ground black
   pepper
1 egg yolk

mrs kirkham's lancashire cheese soufflés

Feeds 4

The majestic taste of Mrs Kirkham's Lancashire cheese is a joy to behold – sharp and tangy, yet at the same time, smooth and creamy. It really is a national treasure. If the word soufflé has set your cooking utensils a-trembling, fear not, for these tasty fellas can be twice baked and, therefore, a doddle. Cook and serve them straight away for a soft, delicate texture or chill them in the fridge for a couple of days after cooking, then reheat for an equally delicious soufflé experience. You can freeze them too, then defrost and reheat and – yep – soufflé heaven. (Obviously don't give the secret away to your guests who will be so impressed with your culinary skill.) To reheat, sprinkle with a little more cheese then reheat for about 8 minutes until heated through.

Preheat the oven to 180°C/Fan 160°C/Gas 4. Grease and flour four 150ml (¼ pint) ramekin dishes. Bring the milk, onion and peppercorns to scalding point in a pan over a medium heat, then strain.

Meanwhile, melt the butter in a saucepan, stir in the flour and cook for 1 minute to create a roux. Now slowly add the flavoured milk, a little at a time, allowing the roux to bubble slightly each time before adding more milk, stirring continuously until you have a smooth, thick sauce.

Take the pan off the heat and beat the egg yolks, thyme and three-quarters of the grated cheese into the sauce. Season to taste.

In a clean, dry mixing bowl, whisk the egg whites until stiff enough to hold soft peaks. Fold one-quarter of the whites into the sauce mixture to lighten it. Gradually fold the remaining egg whites into the sauce, a good spoonful at a time.

Divide the mixture between the ramekin dishes. If you're going to cook the soufflés immediately, sprinkle over the rest of the cheese. If not, keep the cheese and cover and chill the ramekins until you're ready to cook the soufflés.

Put the ramekins into a baking dish filled with water to come about one-third up the sides of the ramekins. Place in the oven and bake for 15 minutes until risen and golden.

I like to serve the soufflés garnished with a little watercress, with maybe a few sun-blush tomatoes and some vinaigrette dressing.

225ml (8fl oz) milk
½ onion, roughly chopped
12 black peppercorns
25g (1oz) butter, plus extra for greasing
25g (1oz) flour, plus extra for flouring
2 eggs, separated
1 tbsp chopped fresh thyme
100g (3½oz) Mrs Kirkham's Lancashire cheese, grated
salt and freshly ground black pepper
watercress, sun-blush tomatoes and vinaigrette dressing, to serve

crumpets with rarebit

Makes about 12 crumpets

225g (8oz) strong white
   bread flour
225g (8oz) plain flour
1 tsp salt
¾ tsp cream of tartar
½ tsp sugar
2 x 7g sachets easy-blend
   dried yeast
500ml (18fl oz) warm water
½ tsp baking powder
140ml (scant ¼ pint) milk,
   warmed

Rarebit topping
200g (7oz) Montgomery
   Farmhouse Cheddar cheese,
   grated
1 egg, lightly beaten
1 tbsp wholegrain mustard
1 tsp Worcestershire sauce
salt and freshly ground black
   pepper

Sift both the flours, the salt and cream of tartar into a bowl and stir in the sugar and yeast. Make a well in the centre and pour in the warm water. Beat well, using a wooden spoon, for 2 minutes, until the batter is smooth, then cover the bowl with a clean tea towel or oiled cling film and leave somewhere warm to rise for about 1 hour, until the batter is light and frothy.

Stir the baking powder into the warm milk, then beat into the crumpet batter. Cover and leave to rest for 20–25 minutes. The consistency should be neither too runny nor too thick.

Spoon the batter into well-greased 7.5cm (3-inch) rings, sitting on a lightly greased, medium-hot griddle or non-stick frying pan.

Cook the crumpets for 3–4 minutes. Little holes should appear on the surface while they cook – if not add a little more warm water to the batter. If the batter is too runny, add more flour to the mixture.

Remove the rings, flip the crumpets over and cook for a further 2–3 minutes until lightly browned and firm to the touch. Cool on a wire rack.

Mix together all the rarebit ingredients. Spoon this mixture on to the crumpets and grill until the cheese bubbles and melts. Serve immediately.

Some of life's biggest mysteries: do UFOs exist, why does my toast always land buttered-side down on the floor when I drop it and how do you make the holes in crumpets? The first two, I can't help you with, but the other we can sort out right now. I've been obsessed with crumpet-making from the first time I got them right. The baking powder making those holes appear in the surface is pure magic. This is a good one for showing off with!

goats' cheese & onion tart

Feeds 4

Pastry
225g (8oz) plain flour
100g (3½oz) butter, diced
1 tbsp chopped fresh lavender
(optional)
1 egg, lightly beaten
a little milk to bind, if needed

Filling
50g (2oz) butter
1 tbsp vegetable oil
4 large Spanish onions, sliced
1 garlic clove, crushed
2 tsp caster sugar
salt and freshly ground black
pepper
2 eggs plus 2 egg yolks
150ml (¼ pint) double cream
100g (3½oz) goats' cheese,
crumbled

To make the pastry, simply pulse the flour and butter together in a food processor until they look like damp breadcrumbs. Add the lavender, if using, then add the egg and a little milk, if needed, to help gather the mixture into a dough. Wrap the dough in cling film and chill for at least 30 minutes.

Preheat the oven to 200°C/Fan 180°C/Gas 6. Roll out the pastry and use to line a greased 20cm (8-inch) tart tin. Chill for 20 minutes.

Cover the pastry with greaseproof paper, press it down into the corners, then weigh the paper down with baking beans. Bake blind for 15 minutes, then remove the paper and baking beans and return the pastry case to the oven for a further 5 minutes until crisp and dry. Reduce the oven temperature to 180°C/Fan 160°C/Gas 4.

Meanwhile, for the filling, heat the butter and oil together in a saucepan, then add the onions, garlic, sugar and seasoning and cook over a low heat for about 20 minutes, or until golden.

Whisk together the eggs, egg yolks and cream in a clean mixing bowl, mix in the onions and then pour into the cooked tart case. Scatter the crumbled cheese over the top.

Bake for 20 minutes until the filling is set firm and golden brown.

No brainer time – pastry, caramelised onions and goats' cheese, what's not to like? This recipe marries the classic French-style onion tart with a sharp hit of crumbled goats' cheese. It is so delicious – try it and see. I like to serve it with a simple fresh herb salad dressed with a dash of olive oil and lemon juice.

goats' cheese fondant with beetroot

Feeds 4

My head chef at Earle, Stevie Mac, made these for me one day when we were 'playing' in the kitchen. It's lovely to be able to do that. It's like giving your kids free reign over the toy box, or letting your dog chew on all of your shoes. For chefs it's great to have time to experiment rather than to constantly prep, prep, prep! Anyway, from first taste to the last, these fondants are addictive and delicious in equal quantities. Good boy Stevie!

Preheat the oven to 200°C/Fan 180°C/Gas 6. Season the beetroot cubes, toss in the oil in a roasting tin, then roast for about 20 minutes until soft. As soon as they come out of the oven, toss the beetroot cubes in the vinegar.

Divide the cheese into four and roll into balls. Roll in flour and then in the almonds – it doesn't matter if the almonds break a bit.

Deep-fry the cheese balls in oil at 180°C for about 4–6 minutes, or until golden.

For the dressing, simply blend all of the ingredients together in a food processor.

To serve, arrange some watercress on serving plates, sit a ball of cheese on top, then scatter a few cubes of beetroot around the cheese. Spoon over the dressing.

250g (9oz) fresh beetroot, peeled and cubed
salt and freshly ground black pepper
75ml (2½fl oz) oil
1 tbsp balsamic vinegar
200g (7oz) soft goats' cheese
about 50g (2oz) flour
200g (7oz) flaked almonds
vegetable oil, for deep-frying
a little watercress, to serve

Dressing
200g (7oz) fresh basil
75g (3oz) smoked almonds
1 garlic clove
100g (3½oz) Parmesan cheese, grated
100ml (3½fl oz) olive oil

baked cherry tomatoes with ricotta & basil

Feeds 6

50ml (2fl oz) olive oil
900g (2lb) cherry tomatoes
  (a mix of yellow, red and plum)
salt and freshly ground black
  pepper
100g (3½oz) fresh breadcrumbs
1 garlic clove, crushed
handful of fresh basil, torn into
  pieces
225g (8oz) ricotta cheese
2 eggs
25g (1oz) plain flour
4 tbsp double cream
1 tbsp pumpkin seeds

Preheat the oven to 190°C/Fan 170°C/Gas 5. Pour the oil into a baking dish large enough to hold the tomatoes in a single layer. Chuck in the tomatoes and roll them around to coat them with the oil. Season well.

Mix the breadcrumbs with the garlic and half the basil, then sprinkle this over the tomatoes.

Beat together the ricotta, eggs, flour, cream, remaining basil and some seasoning, then spoon this mixture over the tomatoes.

Scatter the pumpkin seeds over the top of the tomatoes and then bake for 15–20 minutes until set, puffed and lightly golden.

This is a bit like a savoury clafoutis, which is like a sweet toad in the hole, if that makes the slightest bit of sense! It's great eaten hot, but I do find myself picking at it when it's cold as well. It's lovely served with a crisp, peppery watercress salad with a little balsamic dressing.

parmesan-coated aubergines

Feeds 4

75g (3oz) Parmesan cheese, grated
50g (2oz) fresh breadcrumbs
½ tsp cayenne pepper
65g (2½oz) seasoned flour
2 eggs, beaten
2 aubergines
olive oil, for frying

Salad
16 cherry tomatoes, halved
1 tbsp stoned green olives,
  roughly chopped
1 garlic clove, crushed
3 tbsp extra-virgin olive oil
1 tbsp sherry vinegar
handful of rocket
salt and freshly ground black
  pepper

Mix the Parmesan, breadcrumbs and cayenne in a bowl, then spread on a large plate. Put the flour on another plate and put the eggs in a shallow bowl.

Cut the aubergines widthways into thick rounds, then dip them first in the flour, then the beaten egg, then the Parmesan mixture. Fry in hot oil, in a large pan over a medium heat, for 3 minutes on both sides. Drain on kitchen paper.

Toss all the salad ingredients together and serve spooned over the aubergines.

Aubergines can be so wrong. For example, when they're not seasoned, or not cooked enough so that they taste like bitter sponge, or when they're used as a cop out, rather than as a focal point. These tasty slices are such a good way to use aubergines. They're also simple to prepare and delicious to eat. That's a win-win for me!

baked caerphilly with pecans

Feeds 8

When summer comes around I love a good picnic, but I do get a bit bored with sandwiches and quiche, so these little beauties are ideal. You can eat them hot or cold, with a dollop of chutney, a tasty sausage or, as in this recipe, served with a fresh summery salad.

Preheat the oven to 180°C/Fan 160°C/Gas 4 and grease a deep 8-cup muffin tin.

Put all the cheesy stuff, except the pecans, in a food processor and pulse until quite smooth. Remove the blade and fold in the pecans using a spoon.

Divide the mixture between the muffin cups and level the tops with a palette knife. Bake in the oven for 15–20 minutes, until just set.

For the salad, grate the zest from the orange, then peel the fruit and cut it into segments over a bowl, catching the juice. Whisk together the oil, honey, orange juice and zest for the salad dressing and season well.

Slice the fennel very finely across the bulb on a mandolin, then toss with the orange segments in the dressing. Allow to stand for 10 minutes.

To serve, arrange a little nest of watercress on each plate, turn out the baked cheeses and sit them on top, then pile the salad around the side.

Cheesy stuff
225g (8oz) full-fat cream cheese
225g (8oz) Caerphilly cheese
salt and freshly ground black
   pepper
2 eggs and 1 egg yolk
1 tbsp chopped fresh tarragon
100g (3½oz) pecans, roughly
   chopped

Salad
1 orange
150ml (¼ pint) extra-virgin
   olive oil
1 tbsp runny honey
1 fennel bulb
bunch of baby watercress

asparagus with poached egg

Feeds 4

One of the finest ingredients we grow in Britain is asparagus. There's something magical about these shoots of 'grass' that makes me very excited every year when we get them delivered from Formby or the Wirral. The growers won't get any sort of harvest for the first three years, so it takes a bit of investment to get a crop going. It's best to make this dish during asparagus season, but I will allow you to use the imported stuff during the rest of the year.

To make the dressing, warm the lemon juice with the vinegar and tarragon. Whisk the egg yolks in a basin with the warm lemon juice mixture. Whisk in the melted butter, then season. Cover and set aside.

Blanch the asparagus for 1 minute in boiling water. Brush with olive oil, then cook on a heated, ridged griddle for 2–3 minutes until tender and lightly charred.

Meanwhile, poach the eggs for about 3 minutes, so the yolks are still runny. To serve, lay three asparagus spears on each plate, season, then top with a poached egg. Remove the tarragon from the dressing then spoon the dressing over each egg and dust with smoked paprika. Serve immediately.

12 asparagus spears, trimmed
1–2 tbsp olive oil, for brushing
4 eggs
smoked paprika, to garnish

Hollandaise dressing
juice of 1 lemon
2 tsp white wine vinegar
sprig of fresh tarragon
2 egg yolks
250g (9oz) unsalted butter, melted
salt and freshly ground black pepper

asparagus bread & butter pudding

Feeds 6

Serve this delicious savoury bread and butter pudding in big slabs accompanied by a rocket and tomato salad.

Whisk the eggs and egg yolks together in a heatproof bowl. Heat the milk and cream together in a saucepan until simmering, then whisk into the eggs.

Grease an oblong ovenproof dish, measuring about 23 x 10cm (9 x 4 inches). Butter the brioche, then layer it up in the dish with the asparagus, scattering the cheese mixture and herbs in between each layer. Reserve some of the cheese for the top.

Strain the warmed egg custard into the dish, then set the pudding aside to soak for 20 minutes.

Preheat the oven to 180°C/Fan 160°C/Gas 4. Scatter the reserved cheese over the top of the pudding, then bake for 25–30 minutes until puffed and golden.

Serve cut into generous slabs.

2 eggs and 6 egg yolks
300ml (½ pint) full-fat milk
300ml (½ pint) double cream
18 slices brioche
75g (3oz) butter, softened
450g (1lb) asparagus, blanched and chopped
100g (3½oz) each of pecorino, Cheddar and goats' cheese, grated and mixed together
150g (5oz) chopped fresh herbs (such as sage, chives, tarragon and marjoram)

scouse eggs

Feeds 4

4 eggs
1 onion, finely chopped
1 carrot, peeled and grated
1 garlic clove, crushed
½ tsp chilli flakes
1 tsp dried thyme
1 tbsp vegetable oil, for frying
large knob of butter, for frying
400g (14oz) cooked chickpeas
    (canned are fine)
1 beetroot, peeled and grated
salt and plenty of white pepper
flour, to coat
beaten egg yolk, to coat
dry breadcrumbs, to coat
oil, for deep-frying
Piccalilli, to serve (*see* page 107)

Boil the eggs for 9 minutes, then place immediately in a bowl of cold water to cool.

For the outside mix, gently fry the onion, carrot, garlic, chilli flakes and thyme in the oil and butter until soft.

Blend the chickpeas in a food processor until they are smooth, then mix with the grated beetroot and fried vegetables. Season generously as some of the flavour will be lost in the frying.

Shell the eggs and roll them in the flour.

Wrap the vegetable mixture around the eggs, making sure there are no gaps, and mould into balls.

Roll the coated eggs first in the egg wash, then in the breadcrumbs.

Heat the oil in a deep-fat fryer to 180°C. (Don't worry if you don't have a thermometer, you can easily test the temperature by frying a small cube of bread – if it turns golden brown within a minute, the oil is hot enough.) Carefully lower the eggs into the hot oil and fry them for about 3 minutes, or until golden.

Drain the eggs on kitchen paper and serve hot with a good dollop of Piccalilli.

I love Scotch eggs – they're the guilty pleasure I probably shouldn't admit to enjoying! The nice thing about them is the big flavour on the outside and the eggy surprise on the inside. As with many of my culinary experiments, I've tried, here, to interpret a meaty idea for veggie food, without going down the road of meat substitutes. Now, I can't call these Scotch eggs, so why not Scouse eggs? Unlike Scotch eggs, I think these are better served straight from the fryer, rather than cold.

dill & basil frittata with roasted peppers

Feeds 2

2 red peppers
a little olive oil
4 eggs
100ml (3½ fl oz) single cream
salt and freshly ground black
   pepper
1 tbsp each chopped fresh basil
   and dill
75g (3oz) mature Cheddar cheese,
   grated
vegetable oil, for shallow-frying
pecorino or Parmesan cheese
   shavings, to serve
extra-virgin olive oil, for drizzling

Preheat the oven to 200°C/Fan 180°C/Gas 6. Rub the peppers with olive oil, then place in a roasting tin.

Roast the peppers for about 20 minutes until charred. Remove from the oven and put them into a plastic bag to sweat, then peel off the skins and slice the peppers into thick strips.

Beat the eggs and cream together, then season and add the herbs and cheese.

Heat some oil in a 24cm (9½-inch) frying pan, pour in the egg mixture and cook for 4 minutes, until almost set. Place the pan under a preheated hot grill for 1 minute to finish cooking the frittata.

To serve, cut the frittata into six wedges. Layer up three wedges of frittata with strips of pepper in between on each plate, finishing with frittata. Scatter over some pecorino or Parmesan shavings and drizzle with extra-virgin olive oil.

This is all about presentation: it's an incredibly simple dish to make, but by slicing and stacking the frittata and peppers, you make it look far more difficult than it really is. But you don't need to tell that to anyone.

paneer with coriander chutney

Feeds 8

There is something so satisfying about making your own cheese, it's almost magical watching the curds and whey separating, then pressing it and having a real cheese to eat within just four hours! This dish is lovely wrapped in fennel flatbreads (*see* page 106) with a bit of chopped tomato for the coolest wrap you've ever had.

To make the chutney, simply put all the ingredients in a food processor and blend until smooth.

For the cheese, bring the milk to the boil in a heavy-based pan, stirring to stop it catching on the bottom of the pan.

As soon as the milk comes to the boil, turn the heat right down and add the lemon juice. Stir gently until white curd starts to form – this will only take about 30 seconds. Continue to stir gently, taking care not to break up the delicate curds as they form and grow.

Now take the pan off the heat and pour the cheese and whey through four layers of muslin in a colander set over a large bowl. Tie the muslin, then squeeze out as much liquid as you can manage. Leave to drain over the bowl for 1–1½ hours until all the whey has dripped through the muslin into the bowl.

Keeping the curds wrapped in the muslin, place on a board. Set another board on top and press down to flatten the ball shape into an oblong block. Place a heavy weight (a pan full of water is good) on top of the second board for 30 minutes to compress the cheese.

The cheese will now be ready, so carefully peel off the muslin. You can eat it either as it is, or cook it, which is what we'll do. So cut it into cubes, toss in chilli powder and fry for 1 minute on each side until golden. Serve with the chutney.

2 litres (3 ½ pints) milk
4 tbsp lemon juice
1 tbsp chilli powder
vegetable oil, for frying

Coriander chutney
300g (10oz) fresh coriander
4 green chillies
1 garlic clove
pinch of salt
juice of 1 lemon
2 tsp demerara sugar

flatbread with pea pâté

Feeds 6

Flatbread

1 tsp coriander seeds
250ml (9fl oz) natural yoghurt
1 x 7g sachet easy-blend
    dried yeast
550g (1lb 4oz) strong plain flour
pinch of salt
1 tsp smoked paprika
30ml (1fl oz) olive oil, plus extra
    for greasing the griddle

Pâté

500g (1lb 2oz) fresh or frozen
    peas
300g (10oz) ricotta cheese, well
    drained
1 tbsp chopped fresh mint
1 tbsp chopped fresh thyme
1 fat garlic clove
juice of 1 lemon
75ml (2½fl oz) extra-virgin
    olive oil
chopped fresh mint, to garnish

Dry-fry the coriander seeds, then crush them, just a bit, using a pestle and mortar. Don't turn them into a powder, but also don't leave them tooth-breaking size! Put them into a pan with 100ml (3½fl oz) water and bring just to the boil.

Stir the yeast into the yoghurt in a bowl. Take the pan off the heat and pour the softened coriander into the bowl and stir everything well together.

Sift the flour, salt and paprika into the yoghurt mixture, pour in the oil, then, using your hands, combine everything together and knead into a smooth dough. Cover the bowl with a clean tea towel and leave the dough to prove for 1 hour or until doubled in size. Contrary to popular belief it doesn't have to be somewhere warm, but it helps to speed up the process.

Knock back the dough and divide it into six even-sized pieces. Roll into little balls, then roll out on a floured surface to about 10cm (4-inch) rounds.

To cook the bread, brush with a little oil and place on a preheated griddle pan for about 30 seconds on each side.

To make the pâté, simply combine all the ingredients in a food processor and season well. You can make this smooth or, as I prefer, with a little texture.

Serve a whole bread with a dollop of pâté on top and a drizzle of oil and some more chopped mint leaves.

The older I get, the more I love peas; what a fantastic ingredient they are. Fresh peas are truly majestic, but so, too, are those little frozen gems. Picked, podded and frozen within hours, job's a good 'un – there can't be many better store-cupboard essentials. Peas are great in salads and pasta dishes, hot, cold, warm and, in this recipe, blitzed. This is a really simple yet delicious pâté that, combined with the smoky paprika bread, is a pea-tastic success.

spiced filled aubergines

Feeds 4

There's nothing as versatile as the aubergine: it's big, fleshy, meaty and delicious. But equally, it can be a rubbish ingredient if you don't cook it properly and it ends up tasting like a bitter black sponge. Now, this is a lovely dish, making full use of the aubergine's shape, size and structure. I went to Morocco a few years back and ate my own body weight in aubergines. This recipe is based on the magical time I spent there.

Run a knife around the outer edge of each aubergine half to give a 1cm (½-inch) border, then cut 1cm (½ inch) down into the circle in the middle, scoring the flesh in a criss-cross fashion. Sprinkle with salt, then leave them to sit in a colander for 30 minutes.

Heat the oil in a frying pan and fry the onions and garlic until soft on a low heat.

Cut one thick slice from the centre of each tomato and set aside, then chop the remainder. Add the chopped tomatoes, spices, harissa and currants, with their soaking water, to the pan and cook for 40 minutes, stirring occasionally. Season to taste, then let the mixture cool down. Stir in the parsley.

Preheat the oven to 200°C/Fan 180°C/Gas 6. Rinse the aubergines to remove the salt, then fry them for 2 minutes on each side. Place them in an ovenproof dish and bake for 30 minutes until soft. Remove from the oven and allow to cool, then press down the flesh to form little 'cups' and pack in the spicy onion and tomato mixture.

Put one of the reserved slices of tomato on top of each aubergine and drizzle with a little oil. Put a few tablespoons of water in the baking dish around the aubergines to keep them moist, then return the dish to the oven and cook for a further 25 minutes. Sprinkle with cayenne and more chopped parsley and serve with Greek yoghurt.

2 large aubergines, trimmed and cut in half widthways
salt, for sprinkling
vegetable oil, for frying
3 onions, finely sliced
3 garlic cloves, crushed
4 beef tomatoes
1 tsp ground cumin
pinch of ground coriander
1 big tsp of harissa paste
1 tbsp currants (soaked in ½ cupful boiling water for an hour)
good handful of chopped fresh parsley, plus extra to garnish
pinch of cayenne pepper
Greek yoghurt, to serve

courgette fritters with green olive salsa

Feeds 4

Anything that is deep-fried is pretty hard to resist and deep-frying is also good for those ingredients that can be a little bit boring, like the courgette. The good thing about the humble courgette is that it stays moist when cooked, so these guys have a lovely soft texture in the middle and loads of flavour.

For the fritters, first combine the flour, baking powder, paprika, sugar and seasoning in a bowl.

Beat the eggs and milk together. Gradually pour this into the dry ingredients to form a batter.

Combine the sweetcorn, courgettes, carrot and spring onions in another bowl, then add sufficient batter just to bind them, no more.

Heat some oil in a deep-frying pan, then drop in good spoonfuls of the vegetable mixture. Cook the fritters for 2 minutes on each side, then lift them out with a slotted spoon and drain on kitchen paper. Keep the fritters warm until all the vegetable batter is used up.

To make the salsa, crush the olives gently using a pestle and mortar, then put in a bowl with all the other ingredients. Mix well and serve with the fritters.

Fritters
100g (3½oz) plain flour
1 tsp baking powder
pinch of smoked paprika
15g (½oz) caster sugar
salt and freshly ground black
　pepper
2 eggs
75ml (2½fl oz) milk
75g (3oz) sweetcorn
100g (3½oz) courgettes, grated
1 carrot, grated
6 spring onions, finely chopped
oil, for deep-frying

Salsa
200g (7oz) large, stoned green
　olives
grated zest and juice of 2 lemons
50ml (2fl oz) extra-virgin olive oil
1 garlic clove, crushed
1 tbsp capers
1 tbsp chopped fresh parsley
1 tbsp cooked peas

field mushroom pies

Makes 8 pies

Pastry
225g (8oz) plain flour
1 tsp salt
100ml (3½fl oz) milk and water
combined
75g (3oz) vegetarian suet
beaten egg yolk, to glaze

Filling
600g (1lb 5oz) field mushrooms,
sliced
about 75g (3oz) butter
1 tbsp chopped fresh sage
1 tbsp finely chopped fresh
rosemary
½ tsp each ground nutmeg
and ground allspice
200g (7oz) goats' cheese,
crumbled
2 tsp Tabasco sauce
salt and white pepper

First prepare the filling. Fry the mushrooms in the butter together with all the herbs and spices until soft. Now drain (ideally I like to do this the day before to get them really well drained).

Preheat the oven to 180°C/Fan 160°C/Gas 4. To make the pastry, sift the flour and salt into a bowl. Put the milk and water and the suet into a pan and heat gently until the suet has melted, then bring it just up to the boil. Pour the liquid on to the flour and mix with a wooden spoon to form a soft dough.

Knead the dough quickly until smooth, then divide into eight even pieces and press into eight muffin cups while the dough is still warm, saving a quarter of each piece for the lid. (Keep this reserved pastry covered with a cloth or an upturned basin, to prevent it from hardening before you use it.)

Add the cheese and Tabasco to the now cold and drained mushroom mixture and season well. Divide the mixture between the pastry-lined muffin cups.

Roll out the pastry lids and press on top of the pies. Brush with egg wash, then cut a small steam hole in the top of each.

Bake for 45 minutes until golden.

Warm-water pastry is a lovely thing to make. It's usually made for pork pies, but is absolutely magnificent in this dish with big, strong field mushrooms and tangy goats' cheese. Get a really good load of white pepper into the mix to bring out the flavour of the mushrooms. Serve with pickled onions and a cold beer.

tomato vol-au-vents

Feeds 4

8 puff pastry circles, each about
   7.5cm (3 inches) in diameter
1 egg, beaten
purple cress, to garnish
olive oil, for drizzling
Parmesan cheese shavings, to
   garnish

Filling
2 shallots, finely chopped
25g (1oz) butter
1 garlic clove, crushed
about 36 cherry tomatoes, halved
6 tbsp crème fraîche
1 tbsp chopped fresh marjoram
salt and freshly ground black
   pepper
75g (3oz) pecorino or Parmesan
   cheese, grated

Preheat the oven to 200°C/Fan 180°C/Gas 6. Cut out a 5cm (2-inch) hole in four of the pastry circles.

Brush the four whole pastry circles with beaten egg, then place a 'holey' one on top and brush that with egg. Place the vol-au-vents on a baking sheet and bake for about 12 minutes, until crisp and golden.

Meanwhile, prepare the filling. Gently fry the shallots in butter with the garlic until soft. Add the tomatoes and crème fraîche and cook for 3 minutes, then stir in the marjoram and season to taste. Preheat a moderate grill.

Remove the vol-au-vents from the oven and divide the filling between them, piling it into the centres. Sprinkle with grated cheese and place under the grill for 3 minutes.

Serve the vol-au-vents immediately garnished with purple cress, drizzled with a little olive oil and with some Parmesan shavings scattered over the top.

My nan used to have fabulous parties and as a kid I saw exotic foods I'd never seen before at these occasions. Such a treat (in my mind) were the glamorous vol-au-vents, usually filled with either prawns or something made from Campbell's condensed mushroom soup. To me they were the height of sophistication. Even now, take me to a good boozy do, get me up to the buffet and I'll eat my own body weight in vols. So now it's your turn and you get to use some lovely ingredients.

largeplatefuls

squash ravioli

Feeds 4–6

One of my favourite chefs is Mario Batalli, who owns, along with other restaurants, Babo in Greenwich Village, New York. He does incredible things with all Italian foods, but his pasta is genius. This dish is my tug of the forelock in his general direction – good to eat, full of flavour and, once you've made it, you'll never want to stop.

Put everything for the pasta dough, except the semolina, in a food processor and pulse into a loose ball of dough. (You may need to do this in batches unless you've got a large food processor.)

Turn the dough out on to a work surface dusted with semolina and knead for about 5 minutes until it is smooth and elastic.

Wrap the dough tightly in a polythene bag and set aside to rest for 20 minutes.

Cut the dough into eight balls (as smaller portions are easier to manage).

To create really silky pasta, put each ball of dough through a pasta machine on its thickest setting 10 times. After each pass through, fold the dough in three and turn by 90 degrees. Then, reduce the gauge on the machine down to '5' for ravioli.

For the filling, pulse the squash in a food processor until reasonably smooth, then combine this with the ricotta, Parmesan, sage and seasoning.

Cut the pasta into 7.5cm (3-inch) rounds. Put a small tablespoonful of filling on each round, brush the edge of the round with egg wash, then place another round on top and seal the edges.

Cook the ravioli in boiling salted water for 3 minutes until 'al dente'.

For the sauce, simply melt the oil and butter in a saucepan over a medium heat until the butter foams, add the chestnuts and cook for 5 minutes.

Drain the pasta, reserving a little of the cooking water with it, then toss with the chestnut sauce. Scatter with Parmesan or pecorino shavings before serving.

Pasta dough
700g (1 lb 9oz) 00 grade pasta flour
pinch of salt
4 eggs and 9 egg yolks
some fine semolina to dust and roll

Filling
400g (14oz) roasted, cubed squash (roasted in olive oil with garlic and seasoning)
300g (10oz) ricotta cheese, drained
100g (3½oz) Parmesan cheese, grated
1 tbsp chopped fresh sage
salt and freshly ground black pepper
1 egg, beaten

Sauce
2 tbsp extra-virgin olive oil
100g (3½oz) butter
150g (5oz) vacuum-packed chestnuts, finely chopped
Parmesan or pecorino cheese shavings, to serve

veggie carbonara

Feeds 4

My daughter Flo loves traditional carbonara, so whenever she came to Greens she'd fancy it, but obviously there was no bacon to be had in a veggie restaurant. So I set about making a meat-free version for her. All my team loved it so much we tried it on the menu – with stunning results. Now it's your turn.

Cook the spaghetti in a large pan of lightly salted boiling water for about 10 minutes until 'al dente'.

Meanwhile, bring the cream to just boiling point in a pan, then simmer and reduce by one-third. Stir in the grated cheese, until it melts, then add the mascarpone and crushed garlic and season well.

To serve, drain the spaghetti and divide between four serving bowls, with one egg yolk in each, and a tiny bit of the pasta cooking water. Toss the pasta with the egg yolk.

Add a couple of spoonfuls of the cheese sauce to each bowl and mix well together.

Finally, divide the tomatoes between the bowls, add a handful of spinach and a tablespoon of marjoram to each and toss together. Scatter with Parmesan shavings and serve immediately.

450g (1lb) spaghetti
200ml (7fl oz) single cream
150g (5oz) Mrs Kirkham's smoked Lancashire cheese, grated
100g (3½oz) mascarpone cheese
1 garlic clove, crushed
salt and freshly ground black pepper
4 egg yolks
32 sun-blush tomatoes
4 handfuls of baby spinach
4 tbsp chopped fresh marjoram
Parmesan cheese shavings, to serve

linguine with aubergine caponata

Feeds 4

3–4 tbsp olive oil, for frying
2 aubergines, cut into small
  cubes
2 celery sticks, chopped
1 red pepper, deseeded and
  chopped
1 green pepper, deseeded and
  chopped
400g can chopped tomatoes
75g (3oz) honey
175ml (6fl oz) sherry vinegar
1 tbsp capers (in vinegar),
  drained
100g (3½oz) sultanas
100g (3½oz) pine nuts, toasted
400g (14oz) linguine
10 torn fresh basil leaves
Parmesan cheese shavings,
  to serve (optional)

Heat the oil in a frying pan and fry the aubergine for 3–4 minutes, until coloured, then add the celery and peppers and cook for 4 minutes more.

Now add the tomatoes, honey and vinegar and cook for 10 minutes.

Stir in the capers, sultanas and pine nuts and allow to warm through.

Cook the linguine in a large pan of lightly salted boiling water for about 8 minutes until 'al dente', then drain and divide between four bowls. (I quite like to toss it in a little butter first.)

Stir the basil into the sauce and spoon it over the pasta. Serve with some Parmesan shavings, if liked.

This is a delicious combination, and the star of the show is the caponata. The slightly spicy, slightly 'pickly' sauce is fantastic on its own or with rice, veg, meat or fish, but for a really tasty tea, this pasta serving suggestion is spot on.

beetroot gnocchi with smoked almond pesto

Feeds 4

This dish looks so groovy – pink fluffy clouds and intense dark green pesto. And the taste is even better: a warming, comforting eat. I love this as a 'sitting in front of the telly' dish with Ali and the kids, washed down with a chilled glass of beer. Happy days!

Cook the potatoes in salted boiling water for about 20 minutes until soft. Drain thoroughly, then when cool enough to handle, pass them through a potato ricer or mash using a potato masher until smooth. Add the beetroot and mix together.

Make a well in the centre of the potato and beetroot mixture and beat in the egg and seasoning. Add the flour and mix to form a dough. Turn the dough out and knead it for a few minutes on a floured surface.

Divide the dough into four or five pieces and roll out each one into a 2cm (¾-inch) diameter rope. Cut off pieces of dough at 2.5cm (1-inch) intervals.

Drop the gnocchi into a large pan of boiling water, then when they rise to the top, after a couple of minutes, scoop out and refresh in iced water. (You may need to cook them in batches depending on the size of your pan.) Drain, toss in a little olive oil and keep warm in a covered dish in the oven.

To make the pesto, simply blitz all the ingredients, except the oil, together in a food processor. When combined, drizzle in the oil down the processor's feed tube, with the motor running, to make a loose paste, then adjust the seasoning to taste.

To serve, toss the warm gnocchi with the pesto, scatter some Parmesan cheese shavings on top and garnish with basil leaves.

Gnocchi
600g (1lb 5oz) floury potatoes (such as Russets), cut into large chunks
125g (4½oz) cooked beetroot, puréed
1 large egg
salt and freshly ground black pepper
450g (1lb) plain flour, plus extra for dusting
a little olive oil

Pesto
handful of fresh basil, plus extra to garnish
15g (½oz) pine nuts
25g (1oz) smoked almonds
1 garlic clove
100g (3½oz) Parmesan cheese, freshly grated
about 150ml (¼ pint) extra-virgin olive oil
Parmesan cheese shavings, to serve

mushroom macaroni cheese

Feeds 4

A delicious bowl of mac-cheese is very high on my list of comfort foods. It does everything you want, satisfying taste and texture and making you want to lick the plate when you're done. Adding a load of buttery mushrooms does one thing to the dish – it makes me want it NOW.

Cook the macaroni in a large pan of lightly salted boiling water for about 10–12 minutes until 'al dente'.

Meanwhile, make the cheese sauce. Heat the milk with the bay leaves and bring to scalding point, then remove the pan from the heat. In another pan, melt the butter, stir in the flour and cook the roux gently for 2 minutes, without letting it brown.

Remove the bay leaves from the milk, then start to add the milk, a little at a time, to the roux, stirring all the time over the heat, until all the milk has been used to make a lovely smooth sauce. Reduce the heat and simmer the sauce gently for 3 minutes.

Take the pan off the heat and stir in the grated Cheddar or Gruyère cheese, mustard and seasoning.

Fry the mushrooms in butter until soft, then drain and stir them into the cheese sauce.

Drain the macaroni and stir it into the cheese and mushroom sauce.

Spoon the mushroom macaroni cheese either into a heatproof dish or, if you're showing off, into presentation rings. Sprinkle with pecorino cheese and place under a hot grill until it's golden and bubbling.

250g (9oz) macaroni
200g (7oz) assorted mushrooms (shiitake, brown caps etc), thickly sliced
50g (2oz) butter
40g (1½oz) pecorino cheese, grated

Cheese sauce
850ml (1½ pints) milk
2 bay leaves
40g (1½oz) butter
50g (2oz) plain flour
225g (8oz) mature Cheddar or Gruyère cheese, grated
1 tsp English mustard
salt and freshly ground black pepper

mushroom & mint cannelloni

Feeds 6

550g (1lb 4oz) mixed mushrooms (such as fresh shiitake, brown caps etc), sliced
50–75g (2–3oz) butter, for frying
salt and freshly ground black pepper
150g (5oz) cooked chopped spinach
1 tbsp chopped fresh mint
200g (7oz) ricotta cheese, drained
pinch of ground nutmeg
12 sheets fresh lasagne (blanch first if using dried pasta)
250g (9oz) Roquefort cheese, crumbled
100ml (3½fl oz) double cream
1 egg yolk

Preheat the oven to 180°C/Fan 160°C/Gas 4. Fry the mushrooms in the butter until soft, then season well. Add the spinach and mint, then drain thoroughly to remove excess liquid.

Beat the ricotta with the nutmeg, season well, then combine with the mushroom mixture.

Lay some of the mixture along the long edge of each lasagne sheet, then roll up firmly and sit the cannelloni in a large, buttered ovenproof dish, with the joins underneath. The dish should be big enough to hold all the cannelloni rolls in a single layer. Repeat to use all the pasta and mushroom mixture.

Blend the Roquefort with the cream and egg yolk, then pour over the pasta to cover it.

Cover the dish with foil and bake for 15–20 minutes to heat through.

Remove the foil covering and finish off the dish under a hot grill for 2 minutes until golden and bubbling.

All pasta's great isn't it? I think it's the most versatile ingredient in the world. I do love a nice baked, rich pasta dish, like this one. The cannelloni is soft and tender, the filling is full of flavour and the Roquefort glaze is heavenly. Serve with chopped fresh tomatoes drizzled with olive oil.

nut loaf with mixed pepper sauce & mash

Feeds 4–6

When we took over Greens back in 1990, there was a nut loaf on the menu and it was pretty grim – carroty, nutty, stodgy and a bit tasteless. I promised myself it would never be on the menu again, but then I decided I'd try to re-invent it. The thing is, I love meat loaf – the taste, the texture and the eating – so I used the meaty one to be the starting point of the nutty one, if you see what I mean. The result is fab – moist, tasty and well worth a bash at.

Whisk the egg, milk and mustard together, then pour over the cubed bread in a large bowl. Let it stand for 15 minutes, then mash really well with a fork. Add a little extra milk if needed.

Meanwhile, heat the oil in a pan and sauté the onion and celery until nicely browned. Add the mushrooms to the pan and cook for a few minutes until softened.

Add the vegetables to the soaked bread with the herbs, then add the nuts, fresh breadcrumbs, Tabasco sauce and seasoning and mix well. Gently fold in the egg white, then leave to chill for at least 2 hours, or overnight.

Preheat the oven to 180°C/Fan 160°C/Gas 4. Turn the chilled mixture into a 20 x 13cm (8 x 5-inch) loaf tin brushed with butter and dusted with polenta. Bake for 55 minutes.

Meanwhile, boil the potatoes for the mash and make the sauce. Heat a little oil in a pan and fry the peppers until they are soft, then simply blend until smooth in a food processor with the other sauce ingredients. Pass through a sieve and season to taste.

Drain the potatoes and mash them with the butter and some seasoning.

Allow the nut loaf to stand for 5 minutes after taking it out of the oven, then slice and serve with the pepper sauce and mash.

1 egg
150ml (¼ pint) milk
1 tsp Dijon mustard
300g (10oz) soft white bread, cubed
oil, for frying
1 onion, sliced
3 celery sticks, finely chopped
200g (7oz) brown cap mushrooms, chopped
pinch each of dried thyme, nutmeg, tarragon and basil
handful of finely chopped fresh parsley
225g (8oz) hazelnuts, chopped
700g (1 lb 9oz) pecans, chopped
100g (3½oz) fresh breadcrumbs
1 tbsp Tabasco sauce
salt and freshly ground black pepper
1 egg white, lightly beaten
butter, for greasing the tin
polenta, for dusting the tin

Pepper sauce
oil, for frying
1 red pepper and 1 yellow pepper, deseeded and chopped
5 tbsp olive oil
1 tbsp sherry vinegar
1 tsp sugar

Mash
500g (1lb 2oz) floury potatoes, peeled and cut into chunks
125g (4½oz) butter

pea & bean pilaf

Feeds 4

There are loads of different pilafs and many of them are a bad version of savoury rice. I reckon the key to a good one is the way the rice is cooked. So, I like to wash the rice in constant running water, getting your hands in there to wash all the grains. After that I cover the rice in clean water, add the salt, then let it sit in the fridge for a couple of hours. This seems to give it just the right texture. This pea and bean pilaf is one of my favourites, but feel free to go wild with alternative ingredients.

Melt the butter in a pan, then fry the spring onions until soft. Add the spices and cook out for a further couple of minutes.

Drain the soaked rice and add to the pan, stirring well to coat it with the spiced, buttery onions.

Add the beans and peas, then pour in sufficient water to just cover the rice and bring to the boil.

Cover the pan, reduce the heat and cook gently on a low to medium heat for 12–15 minutes, until the rice is just tender.

Season to taste, stir in the parsley and lemon juice and serve with a generous dollop of Greek yoghurt.

75g (3oz) butter
8 spring onions, trimmed and finely sliced
1 tsp ground allspice
pinch of ground cinnamon
150g (5oz) basmati rice (dry weight), soaked as described in the introduction
250g (9oz) shelled broad beans
250g (9oz) freshly podded peas
salt and freshly ground black pepper
2 tbsp chopped fresh parsley
juice of ½ lemon
Greek yoghurt, to serve

rice & beans

Feeds 4

I've only been to Jamaica once and this dish became my staple diet there – it's a delicious way to serve rice. I was tempted to include this recipe in the book as part of a jerk-spiced sweet potato stew, but I think it stands as a great recipe in its own right, which is why it gets an entry all to itself. Serve it with pretty much anything you like; I'd recommend a cold can of Red Stripe!

Heat the oil in a deep pan and fry the onion until soft, but not coloured.

Add the rice, stir well and add the coconut milk and water. Bring to the boil.

Now add the kidney beans and thyme and simmer, covered, for 15–20 minutes, until the rice is cooked. Season well and serve scattered with coriander.

50ml (2fl oz) vegetable oil
1 onion, finely chopped
300ml (½ pint) long-grain rice (measured in a measuring jug)
400ml can coconut milk
400ml (14fl oz) water
400g can kidney beans, drained and rinsed
3 tbsp chopped fresh thyme
salt and freshly ground black pepper
chopped fresh coriander, to serve

rice & mushroom parcel

Feeds 2

250g (9oz) ready-rolled puff
   pastry
1 egg, beaten

Parcel filling
50g (2oz) basmati rice
pinch of turmeric
grated zest of 1 lemon
50g (2oz) butter
1 onion, finely chopped
600g (1lb 5oz) brown cap
   mushrooms, sliced
1 tbsp each chopped fresh
   parsley and tarragon
2 hard-boiled eggs, chopped
salt and freshly ground black
   pepper
few sesame seeds, to sprinkle

For the parcel filling, cook the rice in salted boiling water with the turmeric and lemon zest for about 12 minutes until just tender, then drain.

Meanwhile, melt the butter in a pan and gently fry the onion and mushrooms for about 5 minutes until soft. Tip into a bowl.

Stir the cooked rice, herbs and chopped hard-boiled eggs into the onion and mushroom mixture and season with salt and pepper.

Cut the pastry into a rectangle measuring 30 x 20cm (12 x 8 inches). Place the filling mixture down the middle of the rectangle, brush the edges of the pastry with beaten egg, then wrap it around to enclose the filling and press the edges together to seal. Roll the parcel over so that the long seam is underneath and brush with egg wash.

Place the parcel on a baking sheet and chill in the fridge for 30 minutes. Preheat the oven to 200°C/Fan 180°C/Gas 6.

Sprinkle the pastry with sesame seeds, then bake for 30 minutes until crisp and golden. Serve hot cut into thick slices.

There's a delicious Russian fish pie called 'koulibiac', which is a rice and salmon dish that's wrapped in puff pastry – a sort of 'fish Wellington', if you will. Now, I'm a bit of a sucker for anything in pastry, so I figured I could make a mushroom version of it, and here it is! I've just used some brown caps for the mushy part, but feel free to use shiitakes, girolles, ceps or whatever fungi you fancy. Serve with rocket leaves and your favourite chutney.

peppered mushroom
& stilton pie

Feeds 4

I don't know when it first happened but, over the years, pies have climbed up the ladder of respectability and are now officially, in my book, cool. No longer do we think of them as a cheap, disappointing product that we eat when there's nothing else around; now they're funky and chunky. I actually think my friend Angela Boggiano's book *Pie* has a lot to do with it. So here's one pie that is irresistible – yum yum!

For the pastry, simply pulse the ingredients together in a food processor to form a dough, adding a little milk if needed. Wrap in cling film and chill for at least 30 minutes.

Now make the filling. Start by frying the onion and mushrooms in hot oil until soft.

Add the tomato purée and cook for 5 minutes, then add the soy sauce, peppercorns and stock. Bring to the boil, then reduce the heat slightly and cook until the liquid has reduced by half. Season to taste.

Divide the filling mixture between four individual pie dishes. Divide the Stilton between the dishes too.

Preheat the oven to 200°C/Fan 180°C/Gas 6. Cut the pastry into four pieces and roll into four circles, just bigger than the dishes.

Damp the rim of the dishes with water and cover the pie dishes with pastry, trim the edges and cut a little hole in the top of each. Brush all over with egg wash to glaze. Bake the pies for about 20 minutes until crisp and golden. Serve with buttery mash and green beans, if liked.

Pastry
225g (8oz) plain flour
100g (3½oz) butter
1 egg
a little milk to bind, if needed
1 egg, beaten

Filling
1 onion, sliced
500g (1lb 2oz) button
    mushrooms, halved
2 tbsp vegetable oil
1 tbsp tomato purée
1 tbsp soy sauce
1 tbsp green peppercorns in
    brine, drained
250ml (9fl oz) vegetable stock
salt and freshly ground black
    pepper
200g (7oz) Stilton cheese,
    crumbled

potato, leek & smoked cheese pies

Makes 4 pies

You really can't beat a good pie and this is a right cracker. I once worked with a lovely lad called Mark on a TV show and he was making cracking hog and apple pies, so this was my veggie version for him to increase the range. It's full of flavour, texture and taste and is great with a selection of pickles, eggs, dill, walnuts and beetroot, and some peppery watercress.

First make the pastry. Sift the flour into a bowl with the salt, then rub in the butter using your fingertips and stir in suet. Add a little cold water to make a dough. Wrap in greaseproof paper or cling film and chill for 30 minutes.

Boil the potatoes for the filling in a large pan of lightly salted boiling water until soft, then drain.

Melt the butter in a frying pan, add the onion, leeks and garlic and fry until softened. Season well and drain on kitchen paper.

Combine all the fried vegetables with the boiled potatoes and the rest of the filling ingredients, then chill in the fridge.

Divide the pastry into four even pieces. Roll out each piece on a lightly floured surface and cut out a 15cm (6-inch) and 7.5cm (3-inch) round from each piece.

Preheat the oven to 200°C/Fan 180°C/Gas 6.

To make each pie, place a mound of the filling in the centre of each large pastry round. Sit the small pastry round on top of the filling, then bring the sides of the large round up and pinch around the top to help it stand. Brush with egg wash, then bake for 20 minutes until golden.

Pastry
225g (8oz) plain flour
pinch of salt
65g (2½oz) diced butter
65g (2½oz) vegetarian suet
1 egg, beaten

Filling
400g (14oz) potatoes, peeled and cubed
large knob of butter, for frying
1 onion, finely sliced
2 leeks, finely sliced
1 garlic clove, crushed
salt and freshly ground black pepper
1 tbsp wholegrain mustard
200g (7oz) smoked Cumbrian farmhouse cheese, coarsely grated

smoked aubergine pudding

Feeds 4

300g (10oz) smoked aubergines, thickly sliced widthways

2–3 tbsp olive oil

450ml (16fl oz) double cream

150ml (¼ pint) soured cream

75ml (2½fl oz) milk

900g (2lb) potatoes, peeled and finely sliced

salt and freshly ground black pepper

1 tbsp chopped fresh dill

125g (4½oz) smoked cheese, grated

Preheat the oven to 200°C/Fan 180°C/Gas 6. Toss the aubergine slices in the olive oil in a roasting tin. Roast for 30 minutes until golden and softened, then drain on kitchen paper. Reduce the oven temperature to 180°C/Fan 160°C/Gas 4.

Warm the two creams and the milk together in a pan.

Arrange a layer of potatoes in the bottom of a large ovenproof dish, season, then layer some of the aubergine slices on top and sprinkle with some dill.

Repeat the layers until all the potatoes, aubergines and dill are used up, pour over the warmed cream mixture, then scatter the cheese over the top.

Bake for 1–1½ hours until soft and gooey.

If you've got a good smokery near to you, then embrace it – sniff around their wares and you'll find some magnificent treats. My local smokery is the Cheshire Smokehouse, and Darren and his team will smoke anything from salt to sausages. I got him to smoke some aubergines for me a while ago and the results were superb – so much so that I've created this recipe to indulge in my love of all things smoked. If, however, you can't get smoked aubergines, then roast ordinary ones with a little smoked paprika. Serve with a herby salad.

vegan lancashire hot-pot

Feeds 6

Sauce
1 tbsp vegetable oil
1 onion, sliced
1 garlic clove, crushed
2 tbsp tomato purée
splash of soy sauce
200ml (7 fl oz) Madeira
200ml (7 fl oz) vegetable stock
2 tbsp barley
1 tbsp chopped fresh thyme
**salt and freshly ground black
    pepper**

Vegetables
3 parsnips
3 carrots
5 celery sticks
200ml (7 fl oz) vegetable stock
**4–6 baking potatoes, peeled and
    finely sliced**
150ml (¼ pint) olive oil

Heat the vegetable oil and fry the onion and garlic until soft. Stir in the tomato purée and cook for a further 5 minutes.

Add the soy sauce, Madeira and stock and bring to the boil, then add the barley. Reduce the heat, cover and cook for 25 minutes, or until the barley is soft.

Peel and chop the parsnips, carrots and celery sticks attractively, then cook them in the stock for about 10 minutes until just tender. Par-boil the potatoes in lightly salted boiling water.

Stir the thyme into the sauce and season to taste. Layer all of the vegetables, except for the potatoes, in six individual pie dishes and spoon over the sauce.

Toss the potatoes in olive oil and season well, then layer these on top of the vegetables.

Place the dishes under a preheated hot grill until the potato topping looks golden and crispy.

This is one of the most popular dishes I've ever created at Greens. With vegan food, it's always a challenge to get both the taste and the texture right. The temptation, when cooking meat-free food, is always to use tons of butter and cream, so when a dish comes together as well as this without those ingredients, it's happy days! I think the key to this dish is the richness of the Madeira, which gives a depth to the sauce. Feel free to vary the veg according to the seasons or taste. Serve with pickled beetroot or red cabbage.

root vegetable & goats' cheese hash

Feeds 6

One of the most regularly asked questions in the kitchen at Greens is: 'What shall we have for tea?' The favourites range from curry, stir-fry and pasta, to toast, chips... and chocolate cake! Then there's always the argument about whose turn it is to cook. Sometimes, though, we have a brilliant tea when we get to experiment, then refuse to tell anybody what's in the stunning new concoction. This is one of my finest tea-time treats that's now a regular on the Greens menu. Serve with Figgy jam (*see* page 109).

Preheat the oven to 200°C/Fan 180°C/Gas 6. Heat the oil in a large roasting tray, then chuck in all the vegetables (except the potatoes) with the garlic and rosemary and roast for about 25 minutes. (If you want to keep the colours clean, roast the beetroot separately.) Season and drain on kitchen paper.

Melt the butter in a frying pan, then fry the potatoes until golden, seasoning well.

Toss the roasted vegetables, basil, pine nuts, gherkins and capers together. Cut the cheese into small cubes and add three-quarters of it to the vegetable mixture.

Divide this mixture between six individual ovenproof dishes and top with the buttery spuds and remaining cheese. Finish for 12–15 minutes in the oven.

150ml (¼ pint) olive oil, for roasting
5 carrots, peeled and cut into 5cm (2-inch) batons
3 parsnips, peeled and cut into 5cm (2-inch) batons
3 red onions, cut into wedges (leave the bottom stalk on to hold them together)
4 beetroot, scrubbed and cut into wedges
1 garlic clove, crushed
4–5 sprigs fresh rosemary
salt and freshly ground black pepper
100g (3½oz) butter, for frying
700g (1lb 9oz) cooked new potatoes, sliced
handful of fresh basil leaves, torn
1 tbsp pine nuts, toasted
4 gherkins, chopped
1 tbsp capers in vinegar, drained
300g (10oz) crumbly goats' cheese

potato, lentil & cauli stew

Feeds 4

2 tbsp vegetable oil
2 onions, sliced
1 garlic clove, crushed
25g (1oz) flour
1 tsp turmeric
200g (7oz) Puy lentils, washed
200ml (7fl oz) red wine (a nice
    Merlot is good)
200ml (7fl oz) vegetable stock
500g (1lb 2oz) waxy potatoes,
    peeled and cut into good-sized
    cubes
250g (9oz) cauliflower, cut into
    big florets
1 tbsp chopped fresh sage
2–3 tbsp wholegrain mustard
juice of 1 lemon
salt and freshly ground black
    pepper

Heat the oil in a large pan, add the onions and garlic and fry until soft.

Stir in the flour and cook for 2 minutes, then stir in the turmeric and lentils and cook for a further 2 minutes.

Now pour in the wine and stock and bring to the boil. When the lentils have boiled for about 5 minutes, add the potatoes and cook for a further 5 minutes, then add the cauliflower. Cook for about 10 minutes until the vegetables and lentils are just tender, but keeping some crunch in the cauli.

Stir in the sage, mustard and lemon juice and season to taste before serving.

I usually use the word casserole, not stew, but some dishes just need to be called a stew. This is everything a 'stew' should be – warming, tasty and very easy to make. It makes you want a cold winter night and a real fire to thoroughly enjoy it. Serve with some crusty bread.

spicyplatefuls

vegetable curry

Feeds 6

500g (1lb 2oz) sweet potato, peeled and cubed

400g (14oz) courgettes, trimmed and cut into 2.5cm (1-inch) rounds

salt and freshly ground black pepper

2 red peppers, deseeded and finely sliced

good handful of baby spinach

Sauce

1 tsp each of cumin, coriander, fennel and fenugreek seeds

2 tbsp vegetable oil

2 onions, sliced

2 garlic cloves, crushed

2 small red birds eye chillies, deseeded and finely chopped

400g can chopped tomatoes

2.5cm (1-inch) piece fresh root ginger, peeled and grated

1 tbsp turmeric

2 cardamom pods, crushed, pods discarded

250ml (9fl oz) vegetable stock

For the sauce, gently toast the cumin, coriander, fennel and fenugreek seeds for 2 minutes in a dry pan, then grind them using a pestle and mortar.

Heat 1 tbsp of the oil in a large pan, add the onions and fry gently for 10 minutes until well coloured. Add the garlic and chilli.

Stir in the tomatoes, ginger, turmeric, cardamom seeds and toasted, ground spices.

Add the stock, bring to the boil and then reduce the heat, cover and simmer for 25 minutes.

Tip the curry sauce into a food processor and blend until very smooth.

Boil or steam the sweet potato until tender.

Toss the courgettes in the remaining oil, then fry them for a few minutes on each side until lightly browned. Season well.

To serve, add all the veggies to the prepared sauce and warm through.

My big sis', Jane, says this is the best curry she's ever eaten. Now I'm not sure how much faith I put in anyone who thinks Barry Manilow, Michael Bublé and the film *Dirty Dancing* are entertaining, but she does make this curry a lot and if she can make it taste good, anyone can (just joking sis')! Serve with steamed rice, naan bread and any other bits you fancy, such as chutney and raita.

individual lentil & egg curry

Makes 4

I tried to think of a funky name for these little pots, as the idea of a lentil and egg combo isn't the most appealing, and does make you worry about what you're doing the next day! The thing is, these are cracking little pots of flavour. The egg gives both an added flavour and a touch of richness to the finished dish. If you want to be very posh, make them in smaller ramekins and use quail's eggs.

In a pan, fry the onion, carrots, celery, garlic and pepper in oil for 10 minutes until soft. Add the curry powder and tomato purée and cook for a further 5 minutes.

Add the lentils and stock, bring to the boil, then simmer for 15–20 minutes until the lentils are soft. Season to taste. Preheat the oven to 180°C/Fan 160°C/Gas 4.

Divide the mixture between four large ramekins or individual pie dishes. Make a well in the centre of each and crack in the eggs. Cover with foil, then cook in the oven for 4 minutes until the eggs are just set.

Sprinkle the curry tops with a pinch of paprika and chopped coriander and serve with warm naan bread.

1 onion, finely diced
2 carrots, finely diced
2 celery sticks, diced
2 garlic cloves, crushed
1 red pepper, deseeded and diced
2 tbsp vegetable oil
1 tbsp hot curry powder
1 tbsp tomato purée
300g (10oz) Puy lentils, washed
600ml (1 pint) vegetable stock
salt and freshly ground black pepper
4 eggs
paprika and chopped fresh coriander, to garnish
naan bread, to serve

falafels

Feeds 6

When I wrote my book *The Accidental Vegetarian* I wouldn't have included falafels because I thought they were a bit too...well...veggie! But trends change and now I find these delicious, fresh Middle Eastern/Mediterranean flavours have become so popular, as has eating small platefuls of food, that they had to be included.

Dry-fry the cumin and coriander seeds in a pan, then grind them using a pestle and mortar.

Put the ground toasted spices, chickpeas, seasoning, baking powder, chilli, garlic, parsley and lemon juice in a food processor and pulse to combine. Mould the mixture into about 30 balls, each about the size of a golf ball.

Heat some oil in a large frying pan and fry the falafels for about 3 minutes until golden all over. Drain on kitchen paper.

Blend the yoghurt with the herbs and lime juice.

Serve the falafels warm with the herb yoghurt and warm pitta bread.

1 tsp each cumin and coriander seeds
500g canned chickpeas, drained, rinsed and patted dry
salt and freshly ground black pepper
1 tsp baking powder
1 red chilli, deseeded and chopped
1 garlic clove, crushed
2 tbsp chopped fresh parsley
juice of ½ lemon
vegetable oil, for shallow frying
pitta bread, to serve

Herb yoghurt
100ml (3½fl oz) Greek yoghurt
1 tbsp chopped fresh coriander
1 tbsp chopped fresh mint
juice of 1 lime

creamed kidney beans & lentils

Feeds 6

500ml (18fl oz) water
250g (9oz) brown lentils, rinsed
½ tsp each cumin and coriander
   seeds
1 tbsp butter, for frying
1 onion, finely chopped
2 garlic cloves, crushed
2.5cm (1-inch) piece fresh root
   ginger, peeled and grated
2 fresh green chillies, finely
   chopped
3 tbsp tomato purée
440g can kidney beans, drained
   and rinsed
salt and freshly ground black
   pepper
75ml (2½fl oz) milk
75ml (2½fl oz) double cream
chopped fresh coriander,
   to garnish
lime wedges, to serve

Heat the water in a saucepan to boiling point, add the lentils and cook for about 30 minutes until soft but still holding their shape.

Dry-fry the cumin and coriander seeds for 4 minutes to release their aroma and flavour. Set aside.

Melt the butter in a large pan, add the onion, garlic, ginger and chillies and cook for 6 minutes until soft.

Stir in the tomato purée and cook for a further 6 minutes, until it begins to turn a dark red colour.

Now add the cumin and coriander seeds, cook for 3 minutes, then add the kidney beans and lentils, seasoning and milk. Bring to the boil, then simmer for a further 6–8 minutes until most of the liquid has been absorbed.

Stir in the cream and taste to check the seasoning. Scatter with coriander and serve with lime wedges.

On the face of it, this dish is a bit too 'worthy' for me as it smacks of brown 70s veggie nosh. But the flavour is so comforting and delicious that it makes me want to wear a kaftan and listen to the Mamas and Papas' greatest hits! Serve with a spiced fragrant rice.

spiced chickpeas with cumin spuds

Feeds 4

Sometimes the best dishes come from accidents or necessity, and this is a great example. It was first created one day when I was experimenting with side dishes and add ons for various dishes and, as is always the case, had a taste and couldn't stop eating it! We eat this at home, for staff tea, with pastry dishes...in fact, we almost eat this combo more often than toast at Greens!

Preheat the oven to 200°C/Fan 180°C/Gas 6. Heat the oil in a roasting tin until it's smoking hot, then chuck in the potatoes, season well and place in the oven to roast.

After 10 minutes, add the cumin and garlic to the potatoes, give the tin a shake, then pop them back in the oven to roast for about another 15 minutes, until crisp and cooked.

Meanwhile, prepare the spiced chickpeas. Heat the oil and gently fry the onion, pepper, celery, garlic and chillies for 10 minutes until soft. Add the paprika and tomato purée and cook for a further 5 minutes.

Add the chickpeas and crème fraîche, season and warm through. Add the spinach and lemon balm.

Serve each person a good spoonful of the chickpeas topped with crispy potatoes.

oil, for roasting
3 baking potatoes, peeled and cubed
salt and freshly ground black pepper
1 tbsp cumin seeds
1 garlic clove, crushed

Spiced chickpeas
1 tbsp vegetable oil
1 red onion, finely chopped
1 red pepper, deseeded and finely chopped
3 celery stalks, finely chopped
1 garlic clove, crushed
2 birds eye chillies, deseeded and chopped
1 tsp smoked paprika
1 tbsp tomato purée
2 x 400g cans chickpeas, rinsed
200ml (7fl oz) crème fraîche
handful of baby spinach
1 tbsp chopped fresh lemon balm

glass noodles with radicchio & ginger

Feeds 4

100g (3½oz) glass noodles
vegetable oil, for stir-frying
2.5cm (1-inch) piece fresh root
  ginger, peeled and cut into
  matchsticks
1 garlic clove, finely sliced
6 spring onions, finely chopped
1 green birds eye chilli, finely
  chopped
12 shiitake mushrooms, finely
  chopped
1 head radicchio, finely shredded
25g (1oz) toasted sesame seed
  paste
3 tbsp light soy sauce
100ml (3½fl oz) vegetable stock,
  hot

Soften the noodles in hot water in a large bowl for 10 minutes. Drain and cut in half using scissors.

Heat the oil in a wok, then add the ginger, garlic, spring onions, chilli and mushrooms and stir-fry for 1–2 minutes. Now add the radicchio and stir-fry for a couple more minutes.

Add the sesame paste, soy sauce and stock, then the noodles, bring to the boil and serve immediately.

A friend first cooked this dish for me and I was immediately blown away by how simple and delicious it was. Although it's not a traditional Chinese dish, it really works as the radicchio gives it a lovely bitterness.

spinach & prune stew

Feeds 4

1 tbsp olive oil
knob of butter
1 onion, sliced
2 garlic cloves, sliced
450g (1lb) fresh spinach, trimmed
4 tomatoes, roughly chopped
150g (5oz) stoned prunes,
  soaked in hot water for
  5 minutes and drained
1 tsp sugar
1 tsp ground coriander
salt and freshly ground black
  pepper
1 tbsp pine nuts, toasted
1 tbsp chopped fresh parsley

Heat the oil with the knob of butter in a large pan, add the onion and garlic and fry until soft and just beginning to colour.

Add the spinach to the pan and cook for 3–4 minutes until just wilted.

Now add the tomatoes, prunes, sugar, coriander and seasoning and cook for 5 minutes until the tomatoes and prunes have softened.

Add the pine nuts and parsley and serve.

Now, I know this sounds weird, but it tastes absolutely fantastic. It's one of those dishes that you simply can't stop eating. It's Persian in origin, hence the sweet ingredients. I love to eat this along with some fragrant pilau rice, scented with rose water and cumin.

pot of noodles

Feeds 4

Noodles are one of the best fast foods around – they're simple, cheap, healthy and versatile. This is a dish that you can adapt to your own liking: you can make it more spicy, more veggie, or less citrussy – it's up to you. The basic instructions are cook 'em fast, make 'em tasty and use whatever you've got in the cupboard.

Cook the noodles in boiling water for 4 minutes until just softened. Drain, toss with a little oil and set aside. Steam the asparagus in a steamer at the same time as you cook the noodles or blanch them in a shallow pan of water for 3–4 minutes until just tender.

Put all the ingredients for the sauce, except the cornflour, into a pan, bring to the boil and cook for 5 minutes. Blend the cornflour with a little cold water to make a paste, then stir into the sauce and cook, stirring, for about 2 minutes until slightly thickened. Keep the sauce warm.

Fry all the veggies in hot oil in a wok until just soft.

Add the noodles to the wok and toss with the veggies. Tip into a serving bowl, pour over the sauce and scatter over the coriander.

400g (14oz) egg noodles
2 tbsp vegetable oil
4 asparagus spears, sliced lengthways
1 red onion, finely sliced
200g (7oz) shiitake mushrooms, finely sliced
1 red pepper, deseeded and diced
1 red chilli, deseeded and chopped
1 tbsp chopped fresh coriander, to garnish

Sauce
150ml (¼ pint) light soy sauce
100ml (3½fl oz) vegetable stock
juice of 2 limes
1 garlic clove, crushed
2.5cm (1-inch) piece fresh root ginger, cut into matchsticks
1 tbsp cornflour

mushrooms with tofu

Feeds 4

My hatred for tofu was well documented in the kitchens at Greens – until I started to deep-fry it. A piece of tasteless tofu is transformed into the tastiest of ingredients with a bit of a bite. This dish is a celebration of tofu.

Cut the tofu into 2.5cm (1-inch) squares. Heat the oil and deep-fry the tofu for a couple of minutes until golden. Remove with a slotted spoon and drain on kitchen paper.

Heat some oil in a wok and stir-fry the garlic and ginger to release their fragrance. Add the mushrooms to the pan and stir-fry until soft. Add the nuts and toss everything together.

Blend together the stock, soy and plum sauces, then pour into the wok and bring to the boil. Simmer rapidly for 3 minutes. Blend the cornflour with a little cold water to make a paste, then stir into the sauce and continue to cook until the liquid has thickened.

Finally add the tofu and serve garnished with some coriander leaves.

200g (7oz) fresh tofu
vegetable oil, for deep-frying and stir-frying
1 garlic clove, crushed
2.5cm (1-inch) piece fresh root ginger, cut into matchsticks
125g (4½oz) shiitake mushrooms, halved
125g (4½oz) oyster mushrooms, cut into large strips
100g (3½oz) unsalted cashew nuts
100ml (3½fl oz) vegetable stock
50ml (2fl oz) light soy sauce
3 tbsp plum sauce
2 tsp cornflour
fresh coriander, to garnish

oriental cottage pie

Feeds 6

115g (4oz) carrots, sliced
vegetable oil, for frying
12 spring onions, diagonally sliced
350g (12oz) shiitake mushrooms, thickly sliced
100g (3½oz) water chestnuts, sliced
1 tbsp chopped fresh coriander

Sauce
2.5cm (1-inch) piece fresh root ginger, peeled and cut into matchsticks
2 garlic cloves, crushed
1 tsp dried chilli flakes
50ml (2fl oz) sherry
300ml (½ pint) vegetable stock
150ml (¼ pint) red wine
75ml (2½fl oz) light soy sauce

Topping
350g (12oz) sweet potato, cubed
75g (3oz) butter
1 tbsp sesame seeds, toasted

Salad
mangetout and red cabbage, shredded
sesame seeds, toasted
chopped fresh coriander

For the topping, cook the sweet potato in a pan of lightly salted boiling water until soft. Drain and mash.

Now make the sauce. Quickly stir-fry the ginger, garlic and chilli, then add the rest of the sauce ingredients, bring to the boil and cook for 10 minutes.

Blanch the carrot slices in a shallow pan of water for 3–4 minutes until just tender. Remove from the pan and drain. Heat the oil in a frying pan and fry the spring onions until they're a little charred, then add the mushrooms, carrots and chestnuts and stir-fry together for a few minutes. Stir in the chopped coriander, spoon over the sauce, then transfer to six individual pie dishes.

Beat the sweet potato mash with the butter and spoon it on top of the pies. Cook under a preheated grill until golden, then sprinkle with sesame seeds.

Toss together all the salad ingredients and serve this alongside the pies.

There's a method in Chinese cookery called 'red cooking', which has big, deep flavours and is used in lots of celebration dishes. However, I've never seen it used with veggies, so I thought I should do it. What you get with this is a rich, succulent dish that will send your taste buds wild. Serve with pickled, spiced cabbage.

potato pancakes with spiced beetroot

Feeds 4–6
(makes about 12 pancakes)

The food of Eastern Europe has often been dismissed as dull, boring and full of cabbage and beetroot. Well, I believe that beetroot is the greatest ingredient in the world, and this baby slaps the little purple beauty into a potato pancake with rich, honey overtones. To complete the Eastern European flavour, I'd serve this with some stir-fried cabbage and dot with chestnuts.

Cook the potatoes in their skins, then peel and pass through a ricer (or sieve) until really smooth.

Add the flour and baking powder to the potatoes in a bowl and season well.

Add the milk a little at a time, stirring to combine, then whisk in the eggs to make a thick batter.

Heat some oil in a 20cm (8-inch) frying pan over a medium-high heat and spoon in a large, heaped spoonful of the batter. Cook for about 1 minute, or until the mixture bubbles up, then turn the pancake and cook for a further minute on the other side.

Remove from the pan and keep warm while cooking the rest of the pancakes, lightly greasing the pan with a little more oil between each one.

For the filling, cut the beetroot into wedges. Heat the oil and butter together in a pan until the butter begins to foam, then add the beetroot. Cook without stirring for a couple of minutes and then toss the wedges.

Next add the honey and let the sweet stuff coat the beetroot. Add the vinegar, nutmeg and seasoning and cook for a couple of minutes, then stir in the spinach and pine nuts.

To serve, spoon some filling on to each pancake and fold over. Finish with a dollop of crème fraîche.

Pancakes
700g (1lb 9oz) potatoes
  (use a floury variety)
125g (4½oz) self-raising flour
1 tsp baking powder
salt and freshly ground black
  pepper
400ml (14fl oz) milk
4 eggs
vegetable oil, for frying

Filling
400g (14oz) cooked beetroot
  (the non-pickled, vacuum-
  packed variety is fine)
2 tbsp vegetable oil
50g (2oz) butter
125g (4½oz) honey
3 tbsp red wine vinegar
pinch of ground nutmeg
big handful of baby spinach
1 tbsp pine nuts, toasted
crème fraîche, to serve

turmeric roulade with harissa stew

Feeds 8

Roulades
125g (4½oz) butter
175g (6oz) plain flour
1 tsp turmeric
750ml (1 pint 7fl oz) warm milk
salt and freshly ground black pepper
10 eggs, separated
big handful of roughly chopped fresh basil

Filling
400g (14oz) ricotta cheese
250g (9oz) baby spinach

Stew
1 onion, chopped
1 garlic clove, crushed
1 tbsp olive oil
1 tbsp harissa paste
2 baking potatoes, peeled and cubed
juice and zest of 1 lemon
1 red pepper, deseeded and chopped
3 tomatoes, chopped
200ml (7fl oz) vegetable stock
500g canned chickpeas, drained, rinsed and cooked
large handful of spinach

Preheat the oven to 200°C/Fan 180°C/Gas 6 and grease and line two Swiss roll tins, each measuring 23 x 33cm (9 x 13 inches).

Start making the roulades. Melt the butter in a pan, add the flour and turmeric and cook for 3 minutes to make a spicy roux. Add the milk to the roux a little at a time, stirring continuously over the heat to make a thick sauce. Season to taste.

Take the pan off the heat and beat in the egg yolks and basil. Whisk the whites until stiff, then fold them into the cooled sauce.

Divide the mixture between the trays and spread it evenly. Bake for 15 minutes until risen and springy. Turn out on to wire racks and leave to cool.

For the filling, season the ricotta with salt and pepper, then spread a very thin layer on each sponge base. Lay the spinach over the top.

Roll up each of the roulades firmly and wrap first in greaseproof paper, then in foil. Chill in the fridge until the following day.

For the stew, first fry the onion and garlic in olive oil until soft. Add the harissa, potatoes, lemon zest and juice, pepper, tomatoes and stock and bring to the boil. Reduce the heat, cover the pan and simmer for 10 minutes, until the potatoes are almost cooked.

Add the chickpeas and spinach to the stew and stir well to heat through.

Reheat the roulades, still wrapped in foil, for about 10 minutes at 180°C/Fan 160°C/Gas 4. Cut each one into thick slices and serve one or two slices on top of each portion of stew.

We do lots of variations of roulades at Greens, but this has been one of the most popular with my customers and chefs alike. The slightly metallic taste of the turmeric seems to bring out all the lovely flavours in the stew, which is also great on its own or with some crusty bread. If you can, make the roulades a day ahead to give them time to set.

puy lentil casserole

Feeds 6

Lentils didn't have a starring role in my first book, *The Accidental Vegetarian*, but, in the time since book one, I find myself drawn more and more to the shiny wee beauties with the subtle nutty flavour – particularly the Puy variety, the king of lentils. This is a very simple dish and, as is so nearly always the case with lentils, it's what you cook them with and how you finish them that makes or breaks them – good stock, a touch of curry spice and fresh lime and mint will always bring out the best in them.

Heat the oil, then fry the onion and garlic until soft. Stir in the paprika, curry powder and lentils and cook for 1 minute, then add the wine. Cook until the wine has reduced to pretty much nothing.

Add the stock and bring to boil, then reduce the heat and simmer gently for 15–20 minutes until the lentils are tender, but still with a little bite. Stir in the red pepper and lime zest.

Meanwhile, brush the aubergines and courgettes with oil and sprinkle with salt and pepper to season. Cook on a preheated griddle on both sides until they are nicely lined.

To serve, arrange the aubergines and courgettes in a shallow dish then spoon the lentils over and top with the boiled samphire and chopped herbs. Scatter the mint leaves and squeeze over the lime juice.

2 tbsp vegetable oil
1 onion, finely chopped
1 garlic clove, crushed
1 tsp paprika
1 tsp curry powder
400g (14oz) Puy lentils, well washed
splash of white wine
750ml (1 pint 7fl oz) strong vegetable stock
1 red pepper, deseeded and finely diced
grated zest of 1 lime and juice of 2 limes
1 aubergine, cut into wedges
2 courgettes, thickly sliced diagonally
oil, for brushing vegetables
salt and freshly ground black pepper
200g (7oz) samphire, boiled
1 tbsp chopped fresh parsley
1 tbsp chopped fresh coriander
12 fresh mint leaves

sweet potato gumbo with cornbread muffins

Feeds 6

2 tbsp vegetable oil
1 red onion, chopped
2 celery sticks, chopped
2 fresh red chillies, deseeded
  and finely chopped
2 garlic cloves, finely chopped
150ml (¼ pint) vegetable stock
400g can chopped tomatoes
24 okra
1 bay leaf
400g (14oz) sweet potato, peeled
  and cubed
100g (3½oz) cabbage, finely
  shredded

Gumbo spice mix
1 tsp each of salt, dried thyme,
  cayenne, dried oregano and
  white pepper

Cornbread
200g (7oz) melted butter,
  plus extra for greasing
300g (10oz) plain flour, sifted
50g (2oz) icing sugar, sifted
300g (10oz) polenta
1 tbsp baking powder
1 egg, beaten
250ml (9fl oz) milk

First make the cornbread. Preheat the oven to 200°C/Fan 180°C/Gas 6 and grease a deep 12-cup muffin tin. Mix the flour, sugar, polenta and baking powder in a bowl, then mix in the egg, milk and butter. Divide the mixture evenly between the muffin cups and bake for 20–25 minutes.

While the cornbread is baking, make the gumbo. Heat the oil in a pan and gently fry the onion, celery, chillies and garlic until soft with the spice mix.

Add the stock, tomatoes, okra and bay leaf and bring to the boil.

Add the sweet potato and cabbage to the pan and cook for 15 minutes, until the potato is tender. Season, discard the bay leaf and serve the gumbo with the muffins, straight from the oven.

The first time I tried gumbo, I realised why cabbage had been invented: the combination of that delicious vegetable with thyme, cayenne, oregano and white pepper is a match made in food heaven. (Try it sometime outside of the gumbo-fest you're about to make.) Once you've slurped up all that delicious stew, you'll need a hunk of cornbread to finish off in style. I love to serve these cornbread muffins straight from the oven, broken open with plenty of butter on them. I'd never admit to it if I saw you in the street, but this dish is also delicious with a buttered crust from a doughy, soft, thick-sliced white loaf. I told you I shouldn't admit to it!

white chilli

Feeds 6

330ml bottle light Mexican beer
2 onions, finely chopped
3 garlic cloves, crushed
2 red peppers, deseeded and
    finely chopped
2 jalapeños, finely chopped
3 smoked chillies, finely chopped
1 tbsp ground cumin
400ml (14fl oz) vegetable stock
bunch of fresh coriander
    (stalks and leaves)
50ml (2fl oz) rice vinegar
pinch of salt
400g each canned cannellini
    and butter beans, rinsed and
    drained
1 tbsp chopped fresh oregano
1 tsp chilli powder
1 tsp smoked paprika
250g (9oz) Cheddar or Asiago
    cheese, grated
lime wedges and coriander
    leaves, to garnish

Put the beer, onion, garlic, peppers, jalapeños, chillies, cumin and stock into a large pan and simmer for 10 minutes.

Blend the coriander, vinegar and salt in a food processor to make a smooth paste.

Add the coriander paste along with the beans to the pan with the spiced onion–chilli mixture, and simmer for 25 minutes.

Add the oregano, chilli powder and smoked paprika to the pan.

Serve sprinkled with grated cheese and garnished with lime wedges and coriander leaves. Also, seeing as you probably bought a pack of six beers to make this, you may as well drink the other five!

I ate a variation of this in Santa Barbara and it was amazing; it looks harmless, but boy-oh-boy it doesn't half pack a punch. After much persuasion, I managed to get some info out of the kitchen staff and was very surprised to learn that they boil, rather than fry, the core ingredients. I'm using pre-cooked canned beans here, but feel free to slave over a massive pan of raw ones if your heart desires.

addons

green beans with vodka

Feeds 4–6

These guys get a slow cook, so they look a bit grey/green in colour, but the vodka glaze is superb. Once you've made them I guarantee you'll be thinking of the many different recipes you can use them in.

Heat the oil in a pan, add the onion and fry until soft. Season, then add one-third of the vodka and all the vinegar. Cook on a high heat to reduce the vodka and vinegar to a glaze.

Add the vodka in two more batches, reducing it down each time, until it is used up.

Add the beans to the pan and just cover them with water. Bring to the boil and boil rapidly for about 35 minutes, until the water has reduced down to form more glaze.

2 tbsp olive oil
1 onion, very finely chopped
salt and freshly ground black
   pepper
200ml (7fl oz) vodka
50ml (2fl oz) white wine vinegar
450g (1lb) green beans, trimmed

very finely sliced portobello mushrooms with crème fraîche

Feeds 4

I have a real aversion to the 'carpaccio of...' syndrome. I mean, who really believes there can be such a thing as a carpaccio of pineapple? Oh, you do? Well, then this dish is a carpaccio of portobello mushrooms. The secret to this is to clean the mushrooms well using a soft brush and a piece of kitchen paper, and then to chill them before slicing.

Chill the mushrooms, then slice them very thinly on a mandolin and arrange, with your best artistic eye, on the serving plates. Sprinkle over the mint.

Season with salt and pepper, then drizzle over the oil and a squeeze of lemon juice. Artfully dollop a spoonful of crème fraîche on each serving.

Serve garnished with some pecorino shavings.

2 large flat portobello
   mushrooms, about 150g (5oz),
   stalks removed
20 fresh mint leaves, finely
   shredded
salt and freshly ground black
   pepper
150ml (¼ pint) extra-virgin
   olive oil
juice of ½ lemon
4 tbsp crème fraîche
pecorino cheese shavings,
   to serve

chickpea mash

Feeds 4

I first made this dish a while ago when I was experimenting with flavoured hummus – Thai spices, English country herbs, and so on. Anyway, I then made this chap, which is more of a vegetable and chickpea purée, and thought it tasted delicious. It's a great alternative to mashed spuds and is very tasty.

Heat the oil in a large pan, add the vegetables and garlic and cook on a low heat until softened.

Add the stock, chickpeas and rosemary and bring to the boil. Simmer for 5 minutes or until the vegetables are tender. Remove the rosemary sprigs, then blend in a food processor with the thyme, until smooth.

Stir in the butter, season well and scoff with anything you like – I recommend some pitta bread or foccacia.

4 tbsp olive oil, for frying
2 celery sticks, finely chopped
1 leek, trimmed and finely chopped
1 onion, finely chopped
2 carrots, finely chopped
1 garlic clove
500ml (18fl oz) vegetable stock
2 x 400g cans chickpeas, drained and rinsed
2 sprigs fresh rosemary
1 tbsp chopped fresh thyme
1 tbsp butter
salt and freshly ground black pepper

okra in yoghurt

Feeds 2 as a meal, or
4 as a starter or snack

The problem with our friend 'Mr Okra' is that he doesn't half get sticky! This is fine in a yummy gumbo, but a bit rubbish in most other dishes. Wouldn't it be great if there was something that would prevent the 'goo'? Well, you'd never guess, there is – and it's called yoghurt! So what we have here is a side dish or light snack that is full of delicious Indian flavours and none of that sticky 'goo' – heaven.

Heat the oil until hot, but not smoking, then add the seeds, curry leaves and chilli.

As soon as the seeds begin to pop, add the onion and cook for 1 more minute, then add the salt, sugar and turmeric.

Add the okra and stir constantly for 6–8 minutes.

Finally add the yoghurt and warm through. Garnish with coriander leaves and serve.

3 tbsp vegetable oil
pinch each of black mustard seeds and fennel seeds
10 curry leaves
1 red birds eye chilli, deseeded and finely chopped
1 red onion, finely chopped
pinch of salt
pinch of sugar
½ tsp turmeric
250g (9oz) okra, sliced into 2cm (¾-inch) rounds
3 tbsp plain yoghurt
coriander leaves, to garnish

fragrant spiced lentils

Feeds 4

vegetable oil, for shallow frying
1 red onion, finely chopped
2.5cm (1-inch) piece fresh root
  ginger, peeled and cut into
  matchsticks
2 fresh red and 2 fresh green
  chillies, deseeded and finely
  chopped
1 lemongrass stalk, finely sliced
300g (10oz) red split lentils,
  washed
400ml (14fl oz) vegetable stock
6 fresh kaffir lime leaves,
  shredded
good handful of fresh coriander,
  chopped
juice of 1 lime

Heat some oil in a pan, add the onion, ginger, chilli and lemongrass and lightly fry until softened.

Add the lentils to the pan, give them a quick stir, then add the stock and bring to the boil. Reduce the heat, cover and cook gently for about 20 minutes, or until the lentils are soft and the stock has been absorbed.

Stir in the kaffir lime leaves, coriander and lime juice and serve.

Nowadays I'm cooking with lentils more and more. These guys have a great kick at the end and are quite addictive. I like 'em with a dollop of Greek yoghurt and some warm flatbread.

fennel flatbreads

Makes 6

At Greens, we have some kind of flatbread, such as puri or paratha, on the menu all the time. This one is a recent addition to our repertoire as we've all become such avid fans of fennel seeds. It's superb served with any curry, but also works well for making stuffed wraps with. My chefs (not me you understand) like it wrapped around chips with chilli sauce and yoghurt!

Dry-fry the fennel seeds for 1 minute in a frying pan, then lightly crush them using a pestle and mortar.

Mix the flour with all the spices in a large bowl. Gradually pour in the water to make a soft dough, then knead for a good 5 minutes until the dough is smooth and no longer sticky.

Cover the bowl with cling film and leave the dough to prove for 30 minutes.

Divide the dough into six even-sized pieces and roll these into balls in the palms of your hands. Then roll out each ball on a lightly floured surface into a 15cm (6-inch) circle.

Heat a lightly oiled frying pan and fry each flatbread for 1 minute on each side until golden brown, making sure the dough is pressed down flat on to the pan.

Remove the flatbread from the pan and keep warm, wrapped in a foil parcel or tea towel or placed in a covered container, until they're all cooked and you're ready to serve them.

25g (1oz) fennel seeds
150g (5oz) plain wholemeal flour
pinch of turmeric
½ tsp each of chilli powder, ground coriander and ground cumin
100ml (3½fl oz) warm water
2.5cm (1-inch) piece fresh root ginger, peeled and grated
vegetable oil, for frying

piccalilli

Makes lots

450g (1lb) baby onions

450g (1lb) small cauliflower
florets

450g (1lb) French beans, topped
and tailed, cut into thirds

1 large cucumber, halved,
deseeded, and cut into
2cm (¾-inch) chunks

350g (12oz) coarse rock salt

750ml (1 pint 7fl oz) white wine
vinegar

175g (6oz) light muscovado sugar

1 tbsp each dried English
mustard powder, ground
ginger, ground turmeric and
mustard seeds

2 garlic cloves, crushed

2 red chillies, deseeded and
chopped

1 tbsp cornflour

50ml (2fl oz) cold water

Put all the vegetables in a large bowl, sprinkle with salt and leave overnight to cure.

The following day, tip the vegetables into a colander and rinse thoroughly under cold running water.

Bring the vinegar, sugar, spices, garlic and chilli to the boil in a large saucepan, add the vegetables, then reduce the heat and simmer for about 10 minutes until the vegetables are just tender.

Mix the cornflour with the water to make a paste, then add this to the vegetable mixture and cook for 3–4 minutes until thickened.

Allow to cool, then pot into sterilised jars, label and cover tightly. The piccalilli will last a good month.

When I was a kid I used to stare in envy at the beautiful yellow delight of piccalilli sticking out of my mum and dad's cheese butties, or sitting alongside a ploughman's lunch. The problem was, I didn't actually like the taste of it – it was too spicy for me then and – yuck! – it had cauliflower and mustard in it. Over time, the boy became a man and, as happened with spinach, I finally fell for the charms of this magical yellow chutney. Welcome to adulthood!

carrot jam

Makes lots

350g (12oz) sugar
200ml (7fl oz) water
400g (14oz) carrots, peeled
   and sliced
juice and grated zest of
   2 oranges
juice of ½ lemon
50ml (2fl oz) rose water
5 cardamom pods, crushed,
   shells discarded
50g (2oz) flaked almonds
salt and freshly ground black
   pepper

Put the sugar in a heavy-based saucepan with the water. Place over a medium heat and bring to the boil, stirring occasionally.

Add the carrots and orange zest and keep the pan boiling for about 6–8 minutes until the liquid becomes syrupy.

Add the rest of the ingredients to the pan and boil for another 6–8 minutes until the jam is thick and sticky and the carrots are tender.

Allow to cool slightly, then pot into sterilised jars, label and cover tightly.

Hold on there before you turn the page; this is one of my favourite recipes in this book. Think of it as a chutney, not a jam, although, when spread on white crusty bread, it is fab. You can serve this with any spicy dish to cool it and it's also good with anything smoky.

figgy jam

Makes lots

2 red onions, sliced
2 tbsp vegetable oil
1 garlic clove, crushed
1 carrot, finely chopped
1 small red chilli
400g (14oz) fresh figs, quartered
400g (14oz) dried figs, chopped
1 tbsp ground cinnamon
1 tsp ground cloves
pinch of freshly grated nutmeg
200g (7oz) demerara sugar
150ml (¼ pint) cider vinegar
salt and freshly ground black
   pepper

Fry the onions in the oil in a large pan until soft. Add the garlic, carrot and chilli and cook for a further 4 minutes.

Now add the fresh and dried figs and spices and cook for 2–3 minutes, stirring as you go.

Add the sugar, vinegar and seasoning. Crank up the heat to bring the jam to the boil, then reduce the heat a notch to prevent it from burning, and simmer for about 12 minutes until thick and jammy.

Allow to cool slightly, then pot into sterilised jars, label and cover tightly.

Pickles and chutneys figure pretty strongly in my house: at any given time you'll find the cupboard stacked full of anything ranging from your classic Branston, through Betty's Tomato Chutney and an artisan Piccalilli to fierce Thai-spiced beasts that hurt and burn...in a good way. This baby is a mild, flavoursome creation that works well, like most chutney, with absolutely everything you can think of.

puddings

pear & almond tart

Feeds 8

Bakewell tart has always been a favourite of mine; I love that sweet almond paste when combined with the jam. This lovely tart is of a similar style, but it makes use of our fantastic British pears, which give it a deliciously gentle taste. I'm suggesting Choccy sauce (*see* page 119) and cream to go with it, but ice cream is just as popular in Rimmer Towers.

To make the pastry, pulse the ingredients together in a food processor, using just a little milk to bind them and to make a soft dough. Wrap this in cling film or greaseproof paper and chill for 30 minutes.

Preheat the oven to 200°C/Fan 180°C/Gas 6. Roll out the pastry and use it to line a greased 20cm (8-inch) tart tin. Chill for a further 20 minutes.

Cover the pastry with greaseproof paper, pressing it down into the corners, then weigh the paper down with baking beans. Bake blind for 15 minutes, then lift out the paper and beans and return the pasty case to the oven for a further 5 minutes until crisp and dry. Reduce the oven temperature to 180°C/Fan 160°C/Gas 4.

Meanwhile, prepare the filling. Cream together the butter and sugar, beat in the eggs one at a time, then add the almonds, flour and lemon zest.

Fry the pears in the butter and sugar until just soft.

Spread the almond filling evenly in the pastry case, then press the pears, flat-side down, into the surface. Bake for 30 minutes until the filling is set.

Pastry
225g (8oz) plain flour
100g (3½oz) butter
25g (1oz) caster sugar
1 egg
a little milk to bind

Almond filling
225g (8oz) butter
225g (8oz) caster sugar
4 eggs
175g (6oz) ground almonds
50g (2oz) plain flour
finely grated zest of 1 lemon

Pears
4 pears, peeled, cut in half
  lengthways and cored
100g (3½oz) butter
75g (3oz) caster sugar

apple & blueberry brown betty

Feeds 4–6

I have to confess, I always thought this lovely dessert was from the States, but when I started researching its origins, I discovered, proudly, that it originally comes from old Blighty. It really is the most simple of puds to make; part crumble and part pie. It traditionally has just apples in it, but I like the added zing of blueberries, as they are now grown in the UK.

Preheat the oven to 180°C /Fan 160°C/Gas 4.

Mix the breadcrumbs, crackers and butter until they are well combined.

Mix together the sugar, cinnamon and nutmeg and the seeds scraped from the vanilla pod.

Spread one-third of the crumb mixture in a buttered 1 litre (1¾-pint) ovenproof dish, lay half the apples and blueberries on top, then sprinkle with half the sugar mixture. Repeat the layers, finishing with a layer of crumb mixture.

Bake for about 25 minutes until the top is browned and crisp and the apples are just soft. Serve with crème fraîche.

125g (4½oz) fresh breadcrumbs
125g (4½oz) crushed cream cracker biscuits
200g (7oz) butter, softened
200g (7oz) demerara sugar
1 tsp ground cinnamon
pinch of ground nutmeg
1 vanilla pod, split lengthways
500g (1lb 2oz) apples (half eating and half cooking varieties), peeled and sliced
100g (3½oz) blueberries
crème fraîche, to serve

apple & elderflower cobbler

Feeds 8

900g (2lb) apples, peeled, cored
    and cut into wedges
150g (5oz) caster sugar
125ml (4fl oz) elderflower cordial

Cobbler topping
225g (8oz) plain flour
pinch of salt
2 tsp baking powder
25g (1oz) demerara sugar
100g (3½oz) butter, cubed
175ml (6fl oz) buttermilk
100g (3½oz) Wensleydale
    cheese, crumbled

Custard
4 egg yolks
25g (1oz) caster sugar
1 vanilla pod, split lengthways
300ml (½ pint) milk
100ml (3½floz) single cream

Preheat the oven to 200°C/Fan 180°C/Gas 6. Toss the apples, sugar and cordial together, then cook in a pan over a gentle heat for about 5 minutes until the fruit is just soft, but still holding its shape. Turn into a large ovenproof dish.

For the topping, pulse the flour, salt, baking powder, sugar and butter in a food processor. When the mixture looks like breadcrumbs, add the buttermilk and pulse again to make a sticky dough.

Spoon dollops of the cobbler mixture on top of the fruit, sprinkle with cheese, then bake for 25 minutes until the topping is crisp and golden.

Meanwhile, make the custard. Whisk the egg yolks in a bowl with the sugar. Scrape the vanilla seeds into the milk in a pan then heat to scalding point. Pour the hot milk on to the eggs, whisk, then return to the pan and heat over a low heat, stirring until the custard thickens to a good consistency. Finally, stir in the cream and serve with the hot cobbler.

My best mate, Martin, who now lives in Thailand, was responsible for my conversion to the joys of fruit and cheese. I always thought it was too weird a combination, and not right – in fact, wrong on all levels! But when you taste that acidic cheesy tang alongside the sweet fruit, well, it's a match made in heaven. Cobblers, if you'll excuse the expression, are also heavenly – a good, scone-like topping for pies, both sweet and savoury. Serve with creamy custard.

banoffee pie

Feeds 8

400g can sweetened condensed
   milk
150g (5oz) digestive biscuits
225g (8oz) walnut pieces
75g (3oz) butter, melted
3 large bananas, chopped
250ml (9fl oz) whipping cream
100g (3½oz) chocolate chips
1 tbsp cocoa powder, sifted
pouring cream, to serve

Caramel sauce (optional)
125g (4½oz) butter
125g (4½oz) soft light brown
   sugar
125ml (4fl oz) coconut milk

Put the can of condensed milk, unopened, in a large pan, cover with water, bring to the boil and boil for 4 hours. (Be sure to keep the pan topped up with boiling water from the kettle.) Remove the pan from the heat and leave to cool. The milk will have caramelised inside the tin to a thick toffee known as 'dulce de leche'.

Crush the biscuits and half the nuts in a food processor, mix with the melted butter, then press the mixture into the base of a 25cm (10-inch) tin.

Open the tin of toffee-milk and combine with the bananas. Spread this mixture over the biscuit base. Cover and chill in the fridge for 30 minutes.

Softly whip the cream, then spread it over the top of the chilled pie.

Scatter the remaining walnuts on top, along with the chocolate chips, and dust with cocoa powder.

To make the caramel sauce, put all the ingredients in a heavy-based pan. Bring to the boil, then cook for 3–4 minutes, until it forms a thick, light golden-brown sauce.

Serve the pie with the caramel sauce and extra pouring cream, if you're feeling wickedly indulgent.

Oh my goodness, this is wrong on all levels. This ageing pop star of a pud just shouldn't be nice, and yet it is. Sickly, sweet, calorific – and yet one taste and you're hooked. In fact, this pudding is like that embarrassing CD in your collection that you'd never admit to owning, yet you love to listen to when no one else is around. So make the pie and slip on the Chris de Burgh CD and it'll be our little secret!

doughnut bread & butter pud with butterscotch sauce

Feeds 6

This pudding started out as a bit of fun, but has since become quite a cult. My mate, the actor Lee Boardman, who is best known for his role as the baddie Jez Quigley in *Coronation Street*, appeared on ITV's *This Morning* programme and had to do a cook-off of his favourite pudding against top chef Phil Vickery. I wrote this recipe for him and he won off the back of it! I knew he would because he tested it the day before and could barely speak to me on the phone, such was his level of ecstasy on trying it. Not only that, he plugged me and my restaurants all the way through the show. Now that's what I call a mate. Be warned – this pud is scarily delicious.

Cut the doughnuts in half horizontally and then across, to form crescent-shaped quarters. Spread the cut sides with butter.

Layer the doughnuts in a large, greased ovenproof dish, sprinkling in between each one with demerara sugar and topping with another layer of sugar.

Beat the eggs and egg yolks with the caster sugar and vanilla extract in a heatproof bowl. Heat the cream to scalding point, then pour on to the egg mixture and stir well.

Pour this custard over the doughnuts, then leave to stand for at least 30 minutes before baking. Preheat the oven to 180°C/Fan 160°C/Gas 4.

Bake the pudding in the oven for 40 minutes, until the custard sets.

Meanwhile, boil the ingredients for the butterscotch sauce together in a heavy-based pan.

Serve big dollops of pud with loads of butterscotch sauce and extra cream.

12 ring doughnuts
200g (7oz) butter, softened
plenty of demerara sugar,
   for sprinkling
3 whole eggs and 3 egg yolks
100g (3½oz) caster sugar
dash of pure vanilla extract
500ml (18fl oz) double cream,
   plus extra to serve

Butterscotch sauce
100ml (3½fl oz) double cream,
   plus extra to serve
100g (3½oz) butter
100g (3½oz) soft dark brown
   sugar

peanut butter puds with choccy sauce

Feeds 8–12

675g (1½lb) plain flour
1 tsp baking powder
1 tsp bicarbonate of soda
pinch of salt
100g (3½oz) butter
225g (8oz) crunchy peanut butter
225g (8oz) caster sugar
2 eggs
200ml (7fl oz) buttermilk
100ml (3½fl oz) milk
1 tsp pure vanilla extract

Choccy sauce
125g (4½oz) butter
125g (4½oz) caster sugar
1 vanilla pod, split lengthways
125g (4½oz) dark chocolate
   (70 per cent cocoa solids),
   broken into pieces
300ml (½ pint) water
20g (¾ oz) cocoa powder

Sift together the flour, baking powder, bicarbonate of soda and salt.

In a separate bowl mix together the butter, peanut butter and sugar using an electric beater. Beat in the eggs, then the buttermilk, milk and vanilla extract.

Fold the flour into the peanut mixture. Preheat the oven to 200°C/Fan 180°C/Gas 6.

Divide the mixture between 8–12 greased individual dariole (castle) moulds, so that each is about three-quarters filled. Place on a baking sheet, transfer to the oven and bake for about 20 minutes, until risen and firm to the touch.

Meanwhile, make the choccy sauce. Place the butter, sugar and seeds scraped from the vanilla pod in a pan and heat until the butter has melted.

Reduce the heat to low, add the chocolate and stir well. Add the water a little at a time. When about half the water has been added to the sauce, stir in the cocoa powder. Continue to cook gently, stirring until all the water has been added and the sauce has a good coating consistency.

Turn out the puds from their moulds and trim the bottoms, if necessary, so they stand up straight. Pour over the choccy sauce and serve.

I'm sorry if you're on a diet, or trying to avoid temptation, or generally just trying to be good – these fellas really are unbelievably evil. I feel like Dr Frankenstein when he created his monster, except that mine is in the shape of the most deliciously wicked pud ever. I'll have mine with clotted cream, please!

chocolate & hazelnut meringues

Makes 12–16 meringues

There's a patisserie on the edge of Place des Vosges in Paris that has the most incredible meringues; they're massive pink, brown, green and white beauties and you can see hoards of Parisians desperately trying to avoid breaking them as they head off to work with a bag-full. For me, a meringue has to be crunchy on the outside and chewy in the middle, like these. The tip with these monkeys is to have the oven higher than you need it until you pop the meringues in, then notch it down.

Preheat the oven to 180°C/Fan 160°C/Gas 4.

Beat the egg whites until stiff peaks form, then whisk in the sugar, 1 tablespoon at a time, with the vinegar, until the mixture is smooth and glossy. Gently fold in the cocoa powder, nuts and chocolate.

Spoon 12 heaps of the meringue mixture on to baking parchment on 2 baking sheets. Place the sheets in the oven, then immediately turn the temperature of the oven down to 150°C/Fan 130°C/Gas 2 and bake the meringues for 45 minutes. They should end up crisp on the outside and chewy in the middle.

For the sauce, gently heat all the ingredients together in a pan, stirring occasionally.

For the filling, whip the cream with the icing sugar and seeds scraped from the vanilla pod. Sandwich the meringues together in pairs with the whipped cream and serve with the sauce over the top.

Meringues
6 egg whites
300g (10oz) caster sugar
1 tsp sherry (or red wine) vinegar
3 tbsp cocoa powder, sifted
150g (5oz) shelled hazelnuts, toasted and chopped
50g (2oz) dark chocolate (70 per cent cocoa solids), grated

Filling
400ml (14fl oz) whipping cream
1 tbsp icing sugar
1 vanilla pod, split lengthways

Sauce
200g (7oz) chocolate hazelnut spread
100g (3½oz) butter
200ml (7fl oz) double cream
2 tbsp hazelnut liqueur

raspberry & cream swiss roll

Feeds 6

This is another classic whose image has been tainted by the inferior versions available, yet there's something very satisfying about making a Swiss roll. Once it's been rolled and dusted with icing sugar, it takes on a whole new appearance. It's a bit like the style-challenged individuals on the programme *What Not to Wear* – it starts as a dowdy sheet of sponge, but ends up so curvy and sexy that you just want to lick it!

Preheat the oven to 200°C/Fan 180°C/Gas 6. Grease and line a 30 x 23cm (12 x 9-inch) Swiss roll tin with greaseproof paper.

Whisk the eggs and sugar until pale and fluffy; the whisk should leave a ribbon trail when it is lifted out of the mixture.

Sift the flour into the mixture and very gently fold it in with a metal spoon until thoroughly blended. Turn into the prepared tin and level out into the corners.

Bake for 7–10 minutes until golden and springy.

While the Swiss roll is baking, prepare a sheet of greaseproof paper on the work surface and sprinkle it with icing sugar.

Turn the Swiss roll out on to the sugared paper and peel off the lining paper from underneath. Turn the sugared paper so that the short side of the cake is towards you.

Trim the edges of the Swiss roll to neaten and make a score mark about 2.5cm (1 inch) in from the front edge. Lay another sheet of greaseproof paper on top and roll up with the paper inside, folding the scored edge in first. Allow to cool. (Rolling the sponge immediately, and allowing it to cool in its rolled shape, prevents it from cracking.)

Carefully unroll the sponge and remove the inside paper. Spread the jam over the top, then the cream.

Lay a row of raspberries along one short edge, roll the sponge over, then repeat until the sponge is fully rolled and all the raspberries are used up.

Lift the Swiss roll on to a serving plate and dust with a little icing sugar.

Sponge
3 eggs
75g (3oz) golden caster sugar
75g (3oz) self-raising flour
icing sugar, to dust

Filling
3 tbsp raspberry jam
150ml (¼ pint) whipping cream, whipped
100g (3½oz) raspberries

stollen

Feeds 6–8

225g (8oz) strong white bread
    flour
pinch of salt
1 tsp mixed spice
1 tsp sugar
7g sachet (about 2 tsp)
    easy-blend dried yeast
200g (7oz) mixed dried fruit
    (including glacé cherries)
25g (1oz) flaked almonds
50g (2oz) butter
100ml (3½fl oz) milk
1 egg, beaten
100g (3½oz) marzipan

Topping
25g (1oz) butter, melted
50g (2oz) icing sugar, sifted

Sift the flour, salt and spice into a large mixing bowl. Stir in the sugar, yeast, dried fruit and almonds and make a well in the centre.

Gently heat the butter and milk until the butter has melted and the mixture is just tepid. Pour into the well in the dry ingredients and add the beaten egg. Mix together to form a soft dough.

Turn the dough out on to a lightly floured surface and knead for about 5 minutes until smooth and elastic, then put the dough back into the bowl. Cover the dough with a clean tea towel or oiled cling film and leave to rise in a warm place for about 1 hour, or until it has doubled in size.

Knock the dough back (bash it on a work surface), then knead it for 3 minutes. Roll it out into an oval of about 23 x 18cm (9 x 7 inches).

Roll the marzipan into a piece of about 18 x 5cm (7 x 2 inches). Place this in the centre of the dough then fold over the sides to seal the marzipan inside.

Place the stollen, joined side down, on a greased baking sheet. Cover and leave somewhere warm to prove (rise again) for 1 hour.

Towards the end of the proving time, preheat the oven to 180°C/Fan 160°C/Gas 4. Bake the stollen for 35–40 minutes until golden.

As soon as the stollen comes out of the oven, brush it with melted butter, then lift it on to a wire rack to cool. When cool, dust thickly with icing sugar.

You know stollen isn't just for Christmas, it can be enjoyed all year round. It's weird, as soon as the shops get the decorations up we all want a bit of marzipan, but then, come Boxing Day, poor old almond paste is relegated to being the poor relation again! Well, mark this page as a diary entry for July and make yourself a jolly good slab of stollen to have with your Pimms while watching Wimbledon.

a load-of-old-balls cheesecake

Feeds 12

Choux pastry
150g (5oz) butter
150ml (½ pint) water
200g (7oz) plain flour
6 eggs
600ml (1 pint) double cream,
   whipped

Cheesecake
225g (8oz) chocolate oat biscuits
   or chocolate digestives,
   crushed
175g (6oz) butter, melted
200g (7oz) dark chocolate
   (70 per cent cocoa solids),
   broken into pieces
1kg (2lb 4oz) cream cheese
6 eggs
150g (5oz) caster sugar
splash of dark rum

Choccy sauce
450g (1lb) dark chocolate, broken
   into pieces
25g (1oz) butter
450ml (16fl oz) double cream
100ml (3½fl oz) dark rum
splash of pure vanilla extract
150g (5oz) caster sugar

For the pastry, melt the butter in a pan, add the water, then bring to the boil. Remove from the heat, add the flour and beat with a wooden spoon until the dough binds together. Return to the heat and beat until the mixture forms a smooth, dry ball. Remove from the heat and allow the dough to cool for 2–3 minutes.

Beat the eggs into the dough, one at a time, to make a smooth and glossy paste. Preheat the oven to 220°C/Fan 200°C/Gas 7.

Put the choux paste into a large piping bag fitted with a 1cm (½-inch) plain nozzle and pipe walnut-sized choux balls on to a greased baking sheet. Bake for 15–20 minutes. Transfer to a wire rack, slit the bases to allow steam to escape, then leave them to cool. Reduce the oven temperature to 180°C/Fan 160°C/Gas 4.

For the cheesecake base, mix together the crushed biscuits and melted butter, then press evenly into a 23cm (9-inch) springform tin.

Place the chocolate in a heatproof bowl over a pan of simmering water. Stir occasionally until melted.

Beat together the cream cheese, eggs and sugar, add the melted chocolate and rum and beat well. Pour the mixture on the biscuit base, then bake for 1 hour until firm. Turn off the oven, open the door slightly and allow the cheesecake to cool completely inside.

For the sauce, put the chocolate in a heatproof bowl with the butter. Slowly bring the cream, rum, vanilla and sugar to the boil in a pan, then pour into the bowl and whisk until the chocolate and butter has melted.

Use a piping bag to pipe the whipped cream through the slit in the base of each ball. Arrange them on top of the cheesecake, using choccy sauce to stick them in place. Serve with choccy sauce poured over.

This is the cake I want you to make me for my birthday (5th May). It's a cheesecake (tick), it's got booze in it (tick), it's got lots of sauce (tick) and it looks and tastes fantastic (double tick). Make sure you wrap it well before you post it, though. It's best made the day before it's served to allow time for it to chill properly.

very naughty baked alaska

Feeds 6

I always thought that this was just a gimmick to show how clever chefs are; 'baked ice cream', what nonsense! My my, though, it works – you truly are a genius Mr Chef. I have to admit that I don't think I'd ever made or tasted it until about a year ago, but it is amazingly delicious, especially when it's as sinful as this one is.

First make the chocolate sauce. Put the butter, sugar and seeds scraped from the vanilla pod into a pan and heat until they melt together. Break the chocolate into pieces and add to the pan with the water and cocoa powder. Cook slowly for 6–8 minutes until a lovely thick sauce forms. Remove the pan from the heat and set aside.

Press the brownies into the bottom of a 20cm (8-inch) round ovenproof dish. Sprinkle over the liqueur, then a couple of spoonfuls of the sauce.

Now put a couple of large scoops of each ice cream on top, then place the dish in the freezer while making the meringue. Preheat the oven to 220°C/Fan 200°C/Gas 7.

Whisk the egg whites with half the sugar in a large, clean bowl until they are stiff, then fold in the remaining sugar.

Spoon the meringue mixture on top of the ice cream to cover it completely. Bake immediately for only 3–4 minutes until the meringue is just golden.

Serve at once with more chocolate sauce, if liked.

4 chocolate brownies
50ml (2fl oz) white chocolate liqueur (or dark rum)
luxury chocolate ice cream
luxury vanilla ice cream

Chocolate sauce
100g (3½oz) butter
100g (3½oz) caster sugar
1 vanilla pod, split lengthways
125g (4½oz) dark chocolate (70 per cent cocoa solids)
75ml (2½fl oz) water
1 tbsp cocoa powder

Meringue
2 egg whites
50g (2oz) caster sugar

white chocolate & strawberry mousse

Feeds 4

750g (1lb 10oz) strawberries, plus extra to decorate
2 tbsp fresh lemon juice
250g (9oz) good-quality white chocolate, broken into pieces
1 tbsp white chocolate liqueur (optional)
7g (¼ oz) powdered vegetarian gelatine
50ml (2fl oz) water
450ml (16fl oz) double cream
25g (1oz) icing sugar
fresh mint sprigs, to decorate
biscotti, to serve

Place half the strawberries in a blender or food processor and purée until smooth. Pass the puréed strawberries through a fine sieve into a bowl and add the lemon juice. Slice the rest of the fruit and add to the purée.

Place the chocolate, and chocolate liqueur if using, in a heatproof bowl over a pan of gently simmering water and leave for about 5 minutes, stirring from time to time, until melted. Meanwhile, sprinkle the gelatine over the water in a cup or small bowl and leave to soak for 5 minutes.

Pour a quarter of the cream into a pan, add the sugar and then warm gently. Add the soaked gelatine and stir for 5 minutes over a low heat until the gelatine has dissolved – do not let the mixture boil.

Pour this cream mixture into the melted chocolate and stir until smooth. Add three-quarters of the strawberry purée.

Pour the remaining cream into a bowl and whip until soft peaks form. Gradually fold the whipped cream into the chocolate and strawberry mixture.

Divide the mixture between four serving glasses, then leave to chill for at least 2 hours or preferably overnight. Chill the remaining strawberry purée too.

Spoon the remaining strawberry purée on top of each mousse and serve with a few crunchy biscotti.

Veggie gelatine is a funny monkey; sometimes it behaves and at other times it seems to have the same setting properties as water! However, in this recipe it always does the job, making the mousse firm, yet yielding. The biggest plus, though, is that this is a delicious pud.

chewy strawberry cookies

Makes about 8 cookies

As my kids have got older, I find that my cooking of sweet things becomes simpler, because we'll tend to make things together. This recipe is such a great one to make with kids: they start with a bowlful of ingredients and end up with cookies – and Dad get's hero status! The dried strawberries are a delight too – allow two hours for them to dry in the oven before starting to make the cookies.

Preheat the oven to 140°C/Fan 120°C/Gas 1. Slice the strawberries, sprinkle with caster sugar, lay on some baking parchment on a baking sheet and place in the oven for about 2 hours, until they dry out.

Remove the dried strawberries and increase the oven temperature to 200°C/400°F/Gas 6.

Cream the butter and muscovado sugar until the mixture is pale and fluffy. Add the egg and seeds scraped from the vanilla pod and mix together.

Fold in the strawberries and the sifted flour and baking powder.

Spoon eight 'blobs' of the mixture on to a baking sheet and bake the cookies for 12 minutes. They should still be soft to the touch when they come out of the oven. Lift on to a wire rack and leave to cool.

175g (6oz) strawberries
1 tsp caster sugar
125g (4½oz) butter, softened
150g (5oz) light muscovado sugar
1 egg, beaten
1 vanilla pod, split lengthways
150g (5oz) plain flour
1 tsp baking powder

chocolate macaroons

Makes 18–20
(9–10 sandwiched pairs)

150g (5oz) ground almonds
300g (10oz) icing sugar
25g (1oz) cocoa powder
4 egg whites

Filling
75ml (2½fl oz) whipping cream
75g (3oz) mascarpone cheese
25g (1oz) icing sugar, sifted
1 vanilla pod, split lengthways

Preheat the oven to 180°C/Fan 160°C/Gas 4 and line two baking sheets with baking parchment.

Blitz the almonds, icing sugar and cocoa powder in a a spice or coffee grinder until very fine.

Whisk the egg whites until they form soft peaks, then fold in the almond mixture.

Spoon the mixture into a piping bag with a 1cm (½-inch) plain piping nozzle and pipe 7.5cm (3-inch) circles on to the baking sheets.

Bake the macaroons for about 10 minutes, with the oven door slightly ajar.

Meanwhile, whisk together all the filling ingredients, including the seeds scraped from the vanilla pod.

Leave the macaroons to cool for a few minutes, then lift on to wire racks using a palette knife and allow to cool completely.

Spread the filling on to the flat side of half the cooled macaroons, then sandwich them together with the remainder. Enjoy!

I was never really bothered about macaroons until I went to a shop/café on Rue de Rivoli in Paris called La Durée, where the selection of macaroons is so amazing – pistachio, licorice, lemon, coconut and more, all of them perfectly formed, then presented in beautifully decorated boxes. Well, I thought, I need to get some of those. So I did, and now, after much faffing around, I've come up with a pretty good recipe for them – and now I'm sharing it with you.

christmas muffins

Makes about 8 muffins

100g (3½oz) self-raising flour

100g (3½oz) plain wholemeal flour

1 tsp baking powder

pinch each of ground cinnamon, ground cloves and ground star anise

2 tsp demerara sugar

50g (2oz) golden sultanas

50g (2oz) glacé cherries

grated zest of 1 lemon

3 tbsp clear honey

75g (3oz) butter

1 egg

125ml (4fl oz) plain yoghurt

125ml (4fl oz) milk

Icing

100g (3½oz) icing sugar, sifted

½ tbsp lemon juice

silver cake decorating balls, to decorate

Preheat the oven to 180°C/Fan 160°C/Gas 4. Sift the flours, baking powder and spices into a bowl, then stir in the sugar, sultanas, cherries and lemon zest.

Melt the honey and butter together. Lightly whisk the egg, yoghurt and milk together, then stir in the melted, sweetened butter. Pour this into the dry ingredients and mix together.

Spoon the mixture into 8–10 paper muffin cases in a deep muffin tin and bake for 20 minutes until well risen and golden brown.

Meanwhile, make the icing. Beat the sugar with the lemon juice and about 2 tablespoons of cold water to make a thick, smooth icing.

Lift the muffins on to a wire rack to cool. When cool, spread the icing on top of them and decorate with silver balls.

My kids are allowed a sticky sweet treat for breakfast after Father Christmas has left our house. It might be a chocolate croissant, a choccy coin from the tree or one of these guys. I'm not a big chocolate fan in the morning, so I made these fellas with the kids last year and they went down a treat on Christmas morning. Hmm, just what I need during the festive season – another job to do!

carrot cake & more

Feeds 10

I was once talking to Jo Jo, my producer on *Something for the Weekend*, about recipes for the show and the subject of carrot cake – which I love – came up. She said that her mum, Sue Strous, made the best carrot cake in the world (we all think our mums are best at something), so we made it. I have to admit it's pretty damn good. Ta Sue x

Preheat the oven to 160°C/Fan 140°C/Gas 3. Prepare two greased and lined 20cm (8-inch) sandwich tins.

Sift the flour, baking powder and bicarbonate of soda together into a large bowl, then add the rest of the cake ingredients and mix well. Divide the mixture between the tins.

Bake the cakes for 30–35 minutes, or until risen and firm to the touch.

Leave to cool for 5 minutes, then turn out on to a wire rack and allow to cool completely before icing.

For the soft cheese icing, beat together the butter, sugar and cream cheese, then scrape in the seeds from the vanilla pod. Spread half the icing on top of one cake, then place the other cake on top and spread with the remaining icing. Dust lightly with cinnamon.

300g (10oz) plain flour
2 tsp baking powder
1 tsp bicarbonate of soda
1 tsp salt
175g (6oz) light muscovado sugar
50g (2oz) walnuts
227g can pineapple, drained and finely chopped
3 eggs
handful of sultanas
2 soft bananas, mashed
175g (6oz) carrots, grated
175ml (6fl oz) corn oil

Soft cheese icing
100g (3½oz) butter, softened
200g (7oz) icing sugar, sifted
100g (3½oz) cream cheese
1 vanilla pod, split lengthways
ground cinnamon, for dusting

coffee & walnut cake

Feeds 12

225g (8oz) unsalted butter, plus extra for greasing
225g (8oz) caster sugar
4 eggs
50ml (2fl oz) strong espresso coffee
225g (8oz) self-raising flour
1 tsp baking powder
75g (3oz) walnuts, chopped

Butter cream icing
125g (4½oz) unsalted butter, softened
200g (7oz) icing sugar, sifted
50ml (2fl oz) strong espresso coffee
12 walnut halves, to decorate

Preheat the oven to 180°C/Fan 160°C/Gas 4. Grease and line two deep 20cm (8-inch) round sandwich tins.

Cream together the butter and sugar until very light and fluffy, then beat in the eggs, one at a time.

Add the coffee to the cake mixture and stir well, then sift in the flour and baking powder and add the nuts. Combine the ingredients together quickly, then divide the mixture evenly between the two tins.

Bake the cakes for 25–30 minutes, until risen and springy to the touch. Leave to cool in the tins for a few minutes, then turn out, peel off the paper and finish cooling on a wire rack.

Meanwhile, make the icing. Beat together the butter and icing sugar until pale and creamy, then beat in the coffee.

Sandwich the two cakes together with half of the butter cream icing, then spread the rest on top of the cake. Decorate with walnut halves and then serve with a cup of tea in a lovely china cup.

When I retire (fat chance), I think I'd like to be one of those grumpy old men who frequent various cafés and eat their own body weight in cakes each week. But I have a criteria – the cafés have to serve tea in a pot, with a china cup, linen napkin, full black and white clad waitresses (young and pretty) and they have to have big fat slabs of coffee and walnut cake on a cake stand just for me!

raisin, pistachio & honey cheesecake

Feeds 12

This is like a cheesecake, but not exactly. Okay, it's a cake made of cheese, but it's got a more silky texture than the average cheesecake because of the ricotta and honey. While it should be served cold, I rather like it at just about room temperature, when it's still a bit squishy. Serve with thick Greek yoghurt.

Preheat the oven to 180°C/Fan 160°C/Gas 4. Combine the biscuits, butter and sugar, then press the mixture into the base of a buttered 25cm (10-inch) springform cake tin.

For the topping, beat together the ricotta and cream cheese, eggs, sugar and honey, then fold in the nuts and golden raisins. Spoon the mixture on to the biscuit base.

Bake the cake for 1 hour until lightly golden brown and firm.

Turn off the oven, open the oven door slightly and allow the cheesecake to cool completely in the oven. When cool, run a knife around the sides to loosen it, release the clip and remove cake from tin.

For the sauce, warm the honey with the nuts in a pan.

Cut the cake into wedges, pour over the warm sauce and serve with thick Greek yoghurt.

Biscuit base
250g (9oz) water biscuits, crushed
125g (4½oz) butter, melted
75g (3oz) demerara sugar

Topping
1kg (2lb 4oz) ricotta cheese
200g (7oz) cream cheese
6 eggs
100g (3½oz) caster sugar
100g (3½oz) honey
200g (7oz) shelled unsalted pistachios, lightly crushed
200g (7oz) golden raisins

Sauce
100g (3½oz) honey
100g (3½oz) shelled unsalted pistachios
thick Greek yoghurt, to serve

tea loaf

Feeds 6

If you ever get the chance to eat at Betty's Tearooms in Yorkshire, jump at it. Betty's is a national treasure, with beautiful pastries, elegant surroundings, great Swiss dishes and an illusion of being transported back to more graceful times. In fact, I went there after I got married for the old wedding breakfast (we had potato rosti, if you're wondering). Anyway, they do brilliant stuff there, including tea loaf, which is where the inspiration for this comes from.

Put the dried fruit and tea in a bowl, cover and leave to soak overnight.

The next day, preheat the oven to 180°C/Fan 160°C/Gas 4. Sift the flour and spices into the fruit mix, add the sugar and egg and mix well.

Spoon the mixture into a greased 450g (1lb) loaf tin, measuring about 9 x 20cm (3½ x 8 inches), and spread it out evenly.

Bake for 1–1¼ hours until the loaf is well risen and firm. Test to check it is cooked by putting a skewer in the centre; if the loaf is cooked the skewer should come out clean.

Leave to cool in the tin for 5 minutes, then turn out on to a wire rack to cool completely.

Serve sliced, spread with unsalted butter and jam and a nice cuppa.

75g (3oz) raisins
75g (3oz) sultanas
75g (3oz) currants
300ml (½ pint) Earl Grey tea
250g (9oz) self-raising flour, sifted
1 tsp ground cinnamon
1 tsp ground nutmeg
200g (7oz) soft light brown sugar
1 egg, beaten

buttermilk & blueberry pound cake

Feeds 8

375g (13oz) plain flour
½ tsp baking powder
pinch of salt
500g (1lb 2oz) caster sugar
225g (8oz) butter, softened
6 eggs
225g (8oz) blueberries
grated zest of 1 lemon
1 vanilla pod, split lengthways
225ml (8fl oz) buttermilk
sifted icing sugar, for dusting

Preheat the oven to 180°C/Fan 160°C/Gas 4. Prepare a greased and lined 23cm (9-inch) springform cake tin.

Sift the flour, baking powder and salt into a bowl, then stir in the sugar.

Place the butter in a separate bowl and beat in the eggs, one at a time. Add the blueberries and lemon zest, scrape in the seeds from the vanilla pod and mix well. Stir in the buttermilk.

Pour the buttermilk mixture into the flour mixture and fold together. Transfer to the prepared tin.

Bake for about 1½ hours until golden brown. Test to check it is cooked by putting a skewer in the centre; if the cake is cooked the skewer should come out clean.

Allow the cake to cool for 5 minutes, then turn out on to a wire rack. Cool completely, then dust with icing sugar before serving.

This is one of the simplest recipes in the book, and one of my favourites. Adding buttermilk to cakes always makes them lovely and moist, and adds a bit of zing to the taste. For a variation, substitute blueberries for raspberries, chocolate chips, coconut... or whatever you fancy. Final tip: if you can't get buttermilk, use yoghurt.

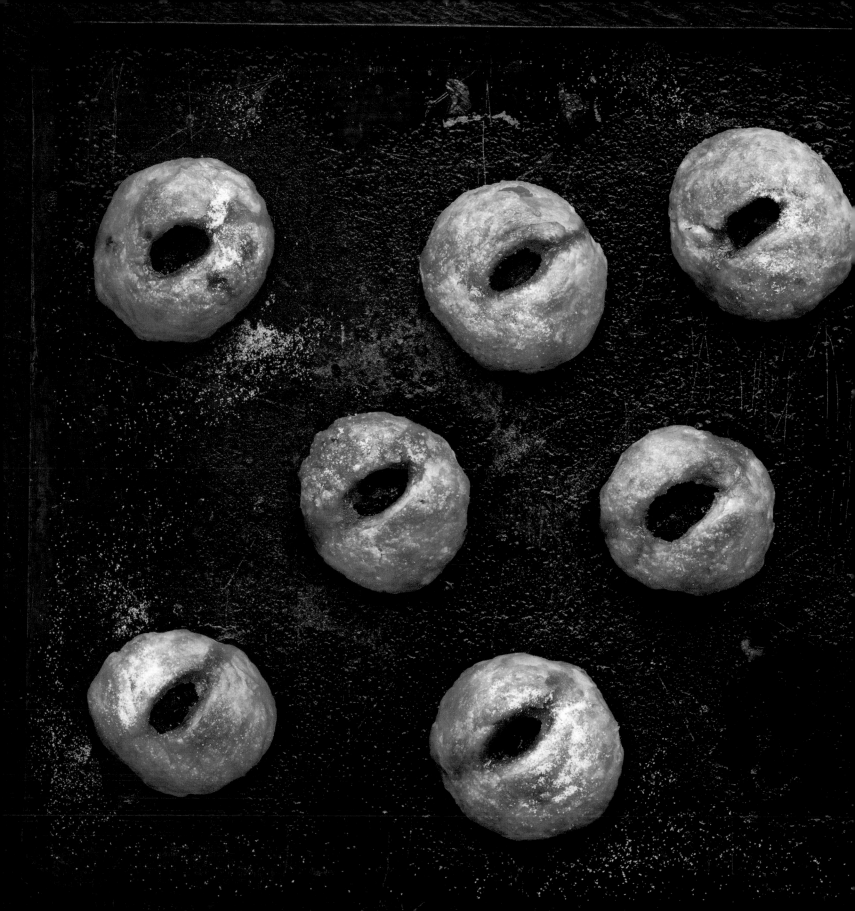

eccles cakes

Makes 18–20

300g (10oz) ready-rolled
   puff pastry
milk, for glazing
caster sugar, for sprinkling

Filling
75g (3oz) butter, melted
150g (5oz) soft light brown sugar
175g (6oz) currants
pinch each of ground cinnamon
   and nutmeg
grated zest of ½ orange

Mix together all the filling ingredients, then set aside. Preheat the oven to 200°C/Fan 180°C/Gas 6

Cut out rounds from the pastry, measuring 8.5cm (3⅓ inches) in diameter.

Put a heaped teaspoon of the filling in the centre of each pastry round. Brush the edges of the pastry with water, then draw them together to the centre, sealing the filling inside and pressing well to secure.

Mould each cake into a neat disc, then turn over so that the pastry join is underneath. Place on a non-stick baking sheet and make a slash on the top of each one.

Brush with a little milk and sprinkle with sugar, then bake for 10–12 minutes until golden brown and puffed up.

Cool on a wire rack and then serve warm.

On the very rare occasion I go on a night out and maybe have one shandy too many, I have a regular hangover cure for the morning after – a full-fat coke, a banana and a warm Eccles cake. Give me the rest of the day in bed and I soon feel as right as rain.

INDEX